NEGLECTED
VOICES

NEGLECTED VOICES

Biblical Spirituality in the Margins

JOHN INDERMARK

UPPER
ROOM BOOKS
NASHVILLE

NEGLECTED VOICES
Biblical Spirituality in the Margins
© 1999 by John Indermark
All rights reserved.

The Upper Room® Website: http://www.upperroom.org

UPPER ROOM®, UPPER ROOM BOOKS™ and design logos are trademarks owned by The Upper Room®, Nashville, Tennessee. All rights reserved.

Scripture quotations not otherwise identified are from the New Revised Standard Version of the Bible, © 1989 by the Division of Christian Education of the National Council of the Churches of Christ in the USA. Used by permission. All rights reserved.

Cover design: Bruce Gore
Cover art: Michael O'Neill McGrath
Second printing: 2000

Library of Congress Cataloging-in-Publication

Indermark, John, 1950–
Neglected voices: biblical spirituality in the margins / John Indermark.
p.   cm.
ISBN 0-8358-0891-2
1. Bible Biography Meditations. 2. Lent Prayer-books and devotions—English.
I. Title.
BS571.I635   1999   97-19599
242'.34—dc21   CIP

Printed in the United States of America on acid-free paper

To

Ruth and Louis Indermark

whose voices still speak and teach

CONTENTS

PREFACE

IN ACTS 19, seven sons of a Jewish high priest named Sceva attempt to exorcise evil spirits by invoking the names of Jesus and Paul. "Jesus I know, and Paul I know," replies the demon, "but who are you?" (19:15). As a result, according to Acts, the possessed man overpowers and wounds them.

Jesus we know, and Paul we know. And probably we know other characters of Old and New Testaments with "name-brand" recognition like David and Sarah or Mary and Peter. But the Bible's cast of characters numbers far more than those we typically study in church school or focus upon in sermons. Does that imply that the minor figures have minor stories, that they are characters of interest only insofar as they shed light on the celebrities of scripture? Absolutely not!

By exploring the lives and stories of lesser-known biblical characters in a six-week series of daily readings, *Neglected Voices* lifts up the spiritual journeys of those who are "out of the spotlight." Characters from three biblical stories form each week's focus (two daily readings per character), with the seventh day's reading making connections with persons and issues of spirituality today.

Persons or groups may use the daily readings of *Neglected Voices* for study and reflection during Lent or another time. Each week organizes itself around a key theme of spiritual growth: Beginnings, Renunciation, Trust, Courage, Servanthood, Promises. The themes reveal a cyclical aspect of spiritual life. For the new to come, we must set old ways aside. To break with the past, trust in God must emerge. To trust radically in God requires courage. To exhibit courage in the light of Christ leads to servanthood.

To exercise self-emptying service relies on the promise of God's reign. The promise of God's reign makes possible new beginnings!

The book's subtitle *Biblical Spirituality in the Margins* underscores that these minor characters, though often overlooked, belong to the Bible's narrative of encounter with God. The narrative of both Hebrew and Christian scriptures means to shape and evoke our own experience of the holy in life. That is why this book speaks of *biblical* spirituality, drawing its characters from both Testaments. Revisiting these "neglected voices" of old intends to tune our ears and spirits to their modern counterparts, voices of faith we might otherwise ignore.

Persons today may discover life in the margins in various places: in voices seldom heard in churches or community who render quiet service; in those who live in places far from the centers of power, whether political or ecclesiastical; in those who get by on humble means, financially or socially. To live in the margins, however, is not to live apart from God. This book on biblical commoners affirms the existence of vital spirituality in persons far removed from the limelight.

Some of you may be part of a study group that uses the accompanying leader's guide to structure your time together. Some of you may belong to a reading group that discusses in one or more sessions the readings in this book without using the leader's guide. Some of you may read this book as part of a daily personal discipline apart from any group experience. I have sought to write in a way that benefits any of these settings. What will be of greatest value, regardless of process, will be your devoting adequate time to read and reflect on the accompanying biblical text along with the day's selection.

Each day offers a biblical text related to the focus character(s), a verse or verses from another text related to that day's theme, the reading itself, and a suggested meditation or prayer. Set aside some time each day for reading and reflection. Later in the day you might review the scripture text and/or selection to discover how your day's experiences have shaped what you read...or vice versa.

Enjoy getting to know these characters. Let them add to your store of biblical knowledge and deepen your sense of the way God works among those in the margins, then and now. And may your own spiritual journey find resonance and growth in the witness of these voices too often neglected.

ACKNOWLEDGMENTS

SOME OF THE voices that go neglected in our lives are the ones to whom we owe thanks. This work owes appreciation and more to a number of persons in my life and ministry.

The good folks at Upper Room Books made it possible for me to bring *Neglected Voices* from idea to manuscript to publication. Editor George Donigian proved a valued guide and advocate in this process with insight and ideas and support. Rita Collett, copy editor by trade and friend from past writing projects, has again helped my work with her careful attention to text and context.

Concurrent with this work's writing, I led a Bible study group at Clatsop Plains Pioneer Presbyterian Church based on the still ongoing manuscript. The group's participation and responses gave encouragement to the overall direction of this work. A significant amount of the leader's guide evolved from those sessions. So to Roy and Dorothy Boyle, Walt Camp, David Carey, Bob and Kay Fackler, Don Hawley, Helen Hoskyns, Gib Marxen, George and Shirley Merrin, Colleen and Howard Simonsen, and Doris and Terry Wheatley—thank you all!

Another group to whom my work on *Neglected Voices* is indebted is the small parishes I have served either in permanent or interim capacities. Small churches, whether rural or town or urban, remain among the most neglected voices in Christendom. Too many still view such congregations as financial anomalies who drain denominational resources or as merely miniature (and therefore diminutive) versions of "full-service" churches. My ministry, both as pastor and writer, has been nurtured by voices of faith alive and well in the ecclesial margins of small churches. This book draws on and affirms their voices.

Neighbors who are colleagues in writing continue over the years to inspire and humble and shape my efforts to practice the craft. Poets and essayists, among them lepidopterist, logger, and archaeologist, keep me engaged in the writing life. Lorne Wirkkala, Jenelle Varila, Pat Thomas, Bob and Thea Pyle, Sue Holway: thank you for constancy of words and friendship.

To Judy Indermark and Jeff Indermark, wife and son, adequate thanks can never be given for the opportunity to pursue this dimension of ministry. The attendant insecurities that accompany writing as profession sometimes can wreak havoc with family life, but my wife and son have kept faith in and patience with me.

And finally, I offer thanks to my mother and father. Dad died in 1983, and Mom is now in her eleventh year of Alzheimer's. In spite of both sets of realities, their voices—as noted on the dedication page—continue to speak and teach in my life. How that is, in my way of thinking, says as much about hope as it does memory. But then, that is getting ahead of the story....

WEEK ONE

⁓

Beginnings

Biblical spirituality presumes the possibility of fresh beginnings in human lives. As simple as that may sound, making that presumption involves an extraordinary act of faith. It cuts against the grain of a portion of biblical tradition. ("Can Ethiopians change their skin or leopards their spots?" [Jer. 13:23]). It violates deeply ingrained folk wisdom on human affairs ("You can't make a silk purse out of a sow's ear"). But a faith devoid of fresh beginnings is a faith devoid of repentance and grace. And a faith devoid of those integral elements of spiritual life is no faith at all.

Day 1

RAHAB

Canaanite, Prostitute, Traitor

JOSHUA 2:1-7

*"Truly I tell you, the tax collectors and the prostitutes
are going into the kingdom of God ahead of you."*
—Matthew 21:31

A MAXIM IN LOGIC states that you can disprove a universal rule by proving an exception to it. People once believed that all mammals bore their young alive rather than by laying eggs. Then came the discovery of the platypus: the exception to that rule. The Third Reich promoted the theory of Aryan supremacy and hoped to showcase its authenticity in the 1936 Olympics in Berlin. Then came Jesse Owens: the iceberg tip for exceptions to that rule.

At first sight Rahab seems the perfect candidate to prove the exception to the spiritual "rule" of fresh beginnings. We might consider the possibility of new starts for most folk—but not for her. Rahab was her day's version of a "three-strikes" felon.

First, Rahab was a Canaanite. In the time of Joshua, Canaanite was not simply an ethnic designation; it became a death sentence. Time and again, Israelite warriors sacking Canaanite towns left no survivors (Josh. 6:21). The equating of Canaanite with idolater might have suggested a "religious" rationalization for the carnage, that of ridding the land of evil. If so, the strategy fared no better than the Flood. Once the waters receded, God saw that the human heart still held evil (Gen. 8:21). In the same way, despite Canaan's fall to the Israelites, shrines and

idols still dotted hilltops and home altars (Judg. 2:11 and following)—but that is another story. Suffice it to say, Rahab as
Canaanite and idolater seems an unlikely candidate for new
beginnings.

This unlikelihood is made all the more exceptional by
Rahab's prostitution. Her house, built into the city wall (Josh.
2:15), provides easy access for customers. The traditions of
Judaism shared nothing of later romantic versions of such persons as "fallen angels" with "hearts of gold." The prophets frequently used harlotry as an image for idolatry in denouncing
Israel's sin (see Hosea). Prostitute added to Canaanite makes the
chances of Rahab's rehabilitation even slimmer.

And Rahab risks universal disdain when she harbors and
protects the Hebrew spies. She lies, she misleads, she deceives
(Josh. 2:4-6). Treason is the operative word for her actions. A
Canaanite author would tell Rahab's story with a much different view than Joshua. Even a neutral observer to the scene
might be more sensitive than Joshua to the repugnance of betray-
ing one's own neighbors and state. Few persons are as despised
as traitors.

So there, in summary, looms the portrait of Rahab: idolater,
prostitute, traitor—a grossly unflattering picture. Presumably
the die is cast for Rahab; there is no turning back for her. She
has gone beyond the point where fresh starts could even be
considered. In a sense, Rahab becomes the patron "unsaint" for
those whom we in the church know have no place among the
righteous. Their crimes are too heinous. Their persons are too
objectionable. Their bridges to us and to God have been
burned...by their own hand and choice. They are our exceptions
to the premise of new beginnings.

Except for one small problem: God. Just when we draw the
lines and establish our decent limits for community, God shows

up, erasing lines and staking new boundaries—with Rahab and her ilk in hand and in heart. Perhaps Rahab, who paved the Israelites' way into Canaan, gave Jesus the idea of prostitutes and tax collectors leading the procession into God's sovereign realm.

But that is getting ahead of ourselves...or is it merely catching up with the premise of new beginnings wrought by God?

For Meditation This Day

Whom have I given up on, O God—and in so doing, assumed you have done the same? Give me patience to wait upon your potential to make all things, even all persons, new.

Day 2

RAHAB

Recognition and Response
JOSHUA 2:8-14; 6:22-25

By faith Rahab the prostitute did not perish.
—Hebrews 11:31

I REMEMBER FONDLY an instructional movie from my childhood school days entitled *Hemo the Magnificent.* Combining animation and real-life sequences, the film depicted the role of blood and the functioning of the human circulatory system. A favorite scene involved an animated figure seated before a control panel (the brain) and a large video monitor (the view taken in by the eyes).

As I recall, a large carnivorous animal suddenly came into

sight. The "controller" recognized the danger and responded by throwing switches to elevate the heart rate to pump more blood, preparing the body for a swift exit. The broader lesson conveyed had to do with the way our senses provide recognition of the world around us so we can respond appropriately.

That linking of recognition and response provides an important insight into far more than physiological functionings of the human body. In terms of the human spirit, recognition and response explain the remarkable transition made from Rahab the sordid to Rahab the faithful, extolled in the "roll call" of faith's exemplars in Hebrews 11. And of continuing interest, the same two words describe how we may still experience fresh starts in our lives.

Recognition discerns the world as it is, not necessarily as it has always been nor even as we think it should be. Rahab saw, as Bob Dylan later sang, that the times they were "a'changin'." Her vision, though, extended beyond historical intuition into the changing fortunes of secular powers. Rahab discerned the hand of Israel's God in events. "I know that the Lord has given you the land…the Lord your God is indeed God in heaven above and on earth below" (Josh. 2:9, 11). Rahab recognizes not only a god involved in human affairs, but *the* God at work in all of creation. The recognition of the world as God's present domain sets Rahab on the path to transformation.

Recognition alone does not guarantee transformation, then or now. It is one thing to see the world as it is. It is another thing to act accordingly. And Rahab responds. Her initial response consists of concealing the Hebrew spies; her actions place her at extraordinary risk with the authorities who seek them. The only plausible explanation for taking such risk resides in her ensuing confession of faith. Only if God's purposes are supreme in this matter will it make sense to act counter to her city's king.

Now the element of risk in faith's response is not peculiar to Rahab alone. Whenever persons are led to discern the world as it truly is—the domain of God—conflict looms with those who prefer versions of the world better suited to their purposes. Crosses and martyrs testify to that conflict. In less severe instances, ridicule of one's choices of values or the tagging of one as "marching to the beat of a different drummer" suffice as motives to enforce conformity to old ways.

But faith will risk response and fresh beginnings, for faith perceives the One to whom "the land" belongs. In Rahab's case, faith responds by invoking sanctuary not merely for self but for others: "my father and mother, my brothers and sisters, and all who belong to them" (Josh. 2:13). Rahab's recognition leads to a fresh beginning not only for herself but for her kin—and, in a curious way, to the potential of fresh beginnings for all humanity. Tucked away in Matthew's genealogy of Jesus we find this extraordinary ancestral detail: "and Salmon the father of Boaz by Rahab" (Matt. 1:5). In Rahab, the premise of fresh beginnings finds provocative demonstration—and gracious hope.

For Meditation This Day

Open my eyes and mind and spirit to your ways, O God; and in their recognition, enable me to respond with faith and courage.

Day 3

SIMEON

Looking Forward

LUKE 2:25-33

But from a distance they saw and greeted
[the promises].
—Hebrews 11:13

VEN WITH THE BEST of peripheral vision, human eyesight takes in no more than a 180-degree view of a 360-degree world. So in every waking moment, we consciously or unconsciously choose which half of the world we will see...and which will remain out of sight. The choice often depends on the task at hand. Walking a twisting mountain trail requires a rather narrow focus on the path immediately ahead with panoramas safely taken in only at rest stops or broad spots. Watching a young child at play takes in a wider picture: at times, drawing sheer delight in her antics; at times, keeping an eye out for any harm or problem; at times, envisioning what she will be and do when she is your age.

Luke describes Simeon as "looking forward"—the actual construction of the Greek word makes "forward looking" an equally plausible translation. In at least one other text from Luke, the line of sight plays a key role. To a would-be follower who first wishes to fulfill obligations "at home" before joining, Jesus says, "No one who puts a hand to the plow and *looks back* is fit for the kingdom of God" (Luke 9:62, *italics added*). Vision determines direction. One cannot move forward without looking forward. One cannot move kingdomward without looking kingdomward.

Simeon looks forward. The 180-degree view of his choosing scans the horizon for "the consolation of Israel." The identity of that consolation comes in the ensuing verse: the promise made of Simeon's not seeing death until he has seen Messiah. Now at this point some might say that Simeon has it made. All he has to do is sit back and wait. He has the promise. But have you ever waited for a promise? How long did you wait—long enough to wonder whether you could trust it? long enough to doubt it would ever come to pass? a day, a week, a month...a lifetime?

Luke does not tell us when Simeon received the promise of Messiah coming into sight. The text hints that Simeon is advanced in years; we do not know his age at the time of the promise. Years of looking forward can sorely test vision. Years of looking forward to peace in Ireland, years of looking forward to racial reconciliation in the United States, years of looking forward to...fill in the blank with all the vigils you have kept.

Several things can happen in vigils. We can exchange the look forward for a look backward by questioning the promise or the promise-maker. We can exchange the look forward for a blindfold by refusing to see what does not conform to our expectations or by retreating into self-absorption. Or the look forward can be maintained. The promise of fresh beginnings can be tenaciously held, even though day after day the eagerly anticipated seems only the agonizingly delayed.

Simeon looks forward with the same tenacity required of all who put their hand to the plow in hopes of God's sovereign realm. No doubt, others in the Temple courtyard had their eyes open that day. Others certainly looked upon the child. But where they may have seen only a cute baby or an interruption of solemnity, Simeon sees nothing less than the future come into view. The tenacity of looking forward climaxes here with the image of aged hands embracing a squirming infant and the resulting peace that comes with promises fulfilled.

Simeon looked forward for what appears in the text almost a lifetime, and God did not disappoint. What of us? Can we keep our 180-degree view focused on God's promises? Vision determines direction. One cannot move forward unless one looks forward. One cannot move Godward unless one looks Godward.

For Meditation This Day

God of the future, when the way seems long, the disappointments overwhelming, and the promises distant, keep my eyes forward that I may see your salvation and find in you my peace.

Day 4

SIMEON

Blessing in Disguise
LUKE 2:34-35

*"Do you think that I have come to bring peace to the earth?
No, I tell you, but rather division!"*
—Luke 12:51

N GEOLOGY, "gradualism" and "catastrophism" offer opposing interpretations on how change occurs. Gradualism argues that geologic change typically takes place in infinitely slow steps over millennia. Water or wind slowly carving into rock, unseen movements beneath the earth's crust—these unobtrusive norms imperceptibly transform the landscape. Catastrophism argues that the most significant geologic change occurs in spurts of extraordinary upheaval. Earthquakes upthrowing ridges and dropping canyons, vulcanism blowing mountains apart in seconds and spewing new islands from magma roiling to the surface—these explosive norms generate earth's landforms.

Simeon comes across as a catastrophist—not geologically but theologically. When he holds the infant in his arms, he sees salvation. But the salvation foreseen does not represent a slow, quiet turning over ages. The fresh beginnings that well up in his mind and voice come in upheaval and division. His words to Mary likely take her breath away: words of falling and rising, of opposition, of a sword piercing her inmost being.

One might wish Luke had written the scene differently. After all, the text indicates that Simeon blesses Joseph and Mary. Why not record the words of blessing, words that seemingly will not offend ear and spirit? Confrontations and crosses will come soon enough. Why not focus on the blessing that will sustain these parents and perhaps their child? Unless, possibly, these words of Simeon *are* the blessing—or part of it.

The text does not rule out either their separation from or inclusion in the blessing. But something in these words is so important that Luke makes a point of recording them. Part of the importance resides in Simeon's perception of salvation unfolding in crisis and contention. One sometimes assumes that those who have lived many years fall into the camp of conservators: those who resist change or who wish to see it proceed at snail's pace. Not Simeon. Perhaps the years of waiting that now see sudden and dramatic fulfillment cause Simeon to see and declare how God's salvation will transform the landscape in cataclysmic ways.

This text joining Simeon to fresh beginnings reveals that new starts do not always proceed in manageable or even welcome ways. We want change on our terms, in our favor. We want salvation that comforts and assures, not disturbs and unsettles.

The church finds in Simeon a difficult visionary. It would be one thing if opposition and division—and piercings of the soul—stemmed from failings and doubtings. It is quite another to hear Simeon pronounce these words as if the road to new beginnings must journey through those unexpected upheavals. We tend to prefer the theology of gradualism, of change slowly emerging and rarely disturbing.

New life, however, sometimes requires an unleashing from the old. And while we will take up this theme more directly in next week's readings, new life already looms clearly on the horizon. Simeon has looked forward for a lifetime to the sight of this child, but his anticipation does not cloud or sugarcoat his vision. So he blesses mother and father—and church—with the insight that the changes will not come easily…but come they will. Even in the disguise of a warning, Simeon pronounces blessing. God's salvation remains sure: even in the midst of division, even in the face of opposition, even in a sword's piercing. For even in such experiences, God can be trusted.

So says the blessing of Simeon. What say you?

For Meditation This Day

Teach me, O God, the way of your Christ—to see, to follow, to trust.

Day 5

BARNABAS

Risking Reputation

ACTS 9:23-28

*You prepare a table before me
in the presence of my enemies.*

—Psalm 23:5

 ONCE HEARD the Presbyterian educator and missionary Kenneth Bailey recount the following story. While teaching at Assiut College in Egypt during the 1960s, Dr. Bailey was arrested. The charge alleged that he did not fill out the required paperwork to allow four foreign students to camp overnight outside his home. If convicted, he faced up to eight years in prison—tantamount, at that time, to a capital sentence. His trial would be held in Luxor, a five-hour journey by train. News of Bailey's situation spread. Area churches withdrew their offers for preaching engagements; hosts canceled dinner invitations; and acquaintances on the street acted as if they had never met.

Then a series of extraordinary events took place. An elder from the church in Assiut said that he would accompany Dr. Bailey on the train to Luxor. The train trip was on a Saturday, with the trial scheduled for Monday. Upon his arrival, the local pastor in Luxor met Dr. Bailey and invited him to preach at his church the next day. And on Sunday evening, the pastor and an elder who owned a street-side cafe on the town square walked arm in arm with Dr. Bailey down the street, into the town square, and sat at one of the cafe's tables. There they served Dr. Bailey a meal in full view of everyone.

The next morning, Dr. Bailey thanked the pastor for going far beyond the call of duty the previous day. He advised the pastor not to go with him to the trial given the current strain of anti-Americanism and the uncertainty of the verdict. The Egyptian pastor replied, "You are my Christian brother, and I must go with you."

In Jerusalem, the appearance of Saul (the name of Paul is not used until chapter 13) generates a crisis among the disciples. Stephen's martyrdom and the ensuing persecution unleashed against the Jerusalem church (Acts 8:1) are fresh in their minds and experience. Saul had witnessed and approved of the martyrdom, and the persecution had taken on a note of ferocity owing to Saul's own hand and methods (8:3; 9:1).

Now, however, the oppressor comes to Jerusalem with claims of having seen the light, figuratively and literally (9:3). Is Saul to be believed? Can the likes of Saul undergo change and renewal? Or is this ploy simply a way to ingratiate himself to the inner circle before snapping a more devastating trap?

The judgment of the disciples is clear: Out of fear, they do not believe him (9:26). Saul as disciple is not worth the risk. Consider for a moment the church's story without Saul/Paul. Would the community of faith be the same without the words of 1 Corinthians 13? Would another have developed the imagery of the church as the body of Christ? Would another have proclaimed the foolishness of the cross or decried the factions of personality?

For all who would see the church as impoverished without Saul, you may thank Barnabas. When the doors seem closed to the risk of Saul's presence in the church, Barnabas risks his own place and reputation (4:36–37). Listen to the actions of Barnabas in 9:27: He "took him, brought him...described for them...." Barnabas serves as the mediator who opens this community— and its former persecutor—to a new beginning. Barnabas does not benefit or make a fresh start himself. Barnabas makes it possible for the church and Saul not only to find each other, but to find *in* each other the grace of God.

Like the Egyptian pastor with Kenneth Bailey, Barnabas stood next to Paul when no one else would take the risk. And from both those risks came new life. Thanks be to God for those who put their own reputation on the line for the sake of others!

For Meditation This Day

For whose sake am I willing to say, "I must go with you"? Whom might I stand beside who might otherwise stand alone?

Day 6

BARNABAS

Making the Best

ACTS 15:36-41

*We know that all things work together for good
for those who love God, who are called
according to his purpose.*
—Romans 8:28

ARTNERSHIPS. FIRST Peter and John in Jerusalem. Now Barnabas and Saul in Antioch and points beyond. Heat forges bonds both of metal and relationship. Barnabas took the heat of standing by Saul in Jerusalem when no other would, no doubt deepening the ties between the two. So when the church in Jerusalem commissions Barnabas to the church at Antioch, Barnabas travels to Tarsus to find Saul, seeking his assistance in the work at Antioch (Acts 11:19-26). Later the pair will undertake a missionary journey to Cyprus.

Two critical developments transform this partnership during this journey. What had heretofore been "Barnabas and Saul" (13:2) now becomes "Paul and his companions" (13:13). The text does not explain the reversal of billing, but the focus of Acts clearly shifts to Paul-no-longer-Saul. Second, almost as a footnote in the verse that introduces this new order, a minor companion named John Mark departs from the entourage in Pamphylia.

Partnerships work in delicate balances, whether among friends, in businesses, or in churches. Does a reversal in the order of names signal a change in the relationship? Not necessarily. Does the departure of a "junior partner" influence the workings of the seniors? Not always. In their initial unfolding, neither of these occurrences causes the writer of Acts to note an explicit change in the partnership.

Yet within two chapters, the partnership ends. Acts traces the cause to the footnoted departure of John Mark. A new journey awaits by Paul's unilateral declaration (15:36). Barnabas desires to take John Mark with them, a desire Paul unilaterally vetoes (15:38). Apparently Paul comes first in more than name order. Disagreement deepens; the partnership dissolves. Great things done by these two will never be done again in tandem. Barnabas and Saul, Paul and Barnabas are no more.

Before we trot out funeral dirges and mourners for a tragic ending, consider the beginnings Barnabas unleashes. Barnabas, once again, risks his own reputation for the sake of a maligned colleague. As with Saul/Paul, Barnabas gives the deserter John Mark another chance. By the act of Barnabas, failure in the church in one instance does not relegate a person to lifelong disgrace—and disuse.

If the truth be told, Barnabas surpasses Paul in this episode by reenacting Jesus' tendency toward ministries of rehabilitation— a ministry that commissioned as apostles the very ones who had deserted him (Matt. 26:56), a ministry that founded a church upon the very one who denied knowing Jesus in a spate of curses (Mark 14:71), a ministry of second chances.

Even the split that sends Barnabas and John Mark in one direction and Paul and Silas in another contributes positively to the church's expansion. Where before one missionary partnership set out to declare the gospel of Jesus Christ, now two sets of partners fan out to do the same, potentially doubling the territory covered and the persons encountered.

So are schisms to be sought? No. Are divisive church conflicts among the abundant cache of personalities and egos within the church to be encouraged? No. But the parting of Barnabas from Paul for the sake of John Mark does reveal God's ability to bring fresh beginnings out of seeming dead ends. In the final analysis, it is not our successes or failures that manage God's purposes but the other way around. Barnabas risked giving Saul a chance, then John Mark a second chance. And God used Barnabas's risks. So it can be for us. May potential endings to what has been not preclude our taking risks for the sake of what could be.

For Meditation This Day

O God, for your forgiving that opens doors for me, I give you thanks. For my forgiving that opens doors for others, I ask your help.

Day 7

MAKING
CONNECTIONS

I am about to do a new thing...do you not perceive it?
—Isaiah 43:19

AN OUTSIDER, an old-timer, and a soft touch: Such a threesome initiates this first week's journey into the biblical margins. Rahab, with her vocation and pedigree clearly outside the respectability camp, complicates our ability to hear of new beginnings. Simeon risks dismissal as one who buries head and hope in some long-past and never-reached promise. And Barnabas? Barnabas fails the modern test of self-promotion. Who will pay attention to one who advocates for others but never for himself?

Yet from the margins these three voices witness to God's ability to create fresh beginnings in the unlikeliest of persons. If they create surprise, it parallels the bewilderment and wonder one encounters in the ministry of Jesus Christ. Time and again those whom Jesus gathers and sends, heals and pardons, are the spiritual cousins of these three: thieves on crosses, disciples who deny, sinners and publicans, those who mourn promises buried for dead among garden tombs. Rahab, Simeon, and Barnabas merit hearing because their voices match those unleashed by Jesus. Likewise, Rahab, Simeon, and Barnabas deserve listening for the sake of discerning their modern-day counterparts among us.

Rahab's voice testifies to how new beginnings must come from recognition of the world as it is and appropriate response. An understanding of the world as it is cannot always (or often?) be gleaned from center stage spokespersons of society, not to mention what constitutes appropriate responses. Those in positions of power, be it political, ecclesiastical, or economic, sometimes have too much at stake to recognize change and welcome fresh starts. It fell not to Jericho's king but to its prostitute to see God's hand in changing circumstances—and she aligns herself accordingly. Listening for new beginnings today extends our hearing to those who tell the truth about how things are—not simply how we want them to be. At times we can hear those voices only in the margins.

Simeon's voice waited with patience for God's new beginning in Messiah's coming. The virtuosity of patience bears remembering in an age where we transmit information instantaneously through optic fibers and expect overnight success in churches, businesses, and sports teams. In part we might trace the rapid turnover of pastors, CEOs, and coaches to this unwillingness to wait. Yet Simeon waits and waits and waits, because the promise depends on God, not on himself.

Who reminds us that new beginnings do not always come on our schedules—that we do not even make the schedules God keeps? Where on the margins of our breakneck-speed society do we hear echoes of Simeon's patience? Listen to those voices. Wait.

And in the meantime, heed the voice of Barnabas: the voice that seeks new beginnings for others, particularly those who otherwise go unspoken for. Personal status can serve as a compelling human motive. To elevate or maintain one's place can consume the ambitious. So it is refreshing, or perhaps it is seditious, to see Barnabas acting, oblivious to issues of his own standing, to ensure that others receive a chance. That is not how you get ahead, that is not how you advance; but that is how you serve. New beginnings are not always self-defined, much less self-serving. Whom do you see speaking and embodying that voice today in your church, in your community, in your family? Listen and learn, for from them God still brings new beginnings.

Biblical spirituality presumes the possibility of fresh beginnings. But presumptions alone do not bring them into being. God works through the likes of Rahab and Simeon and Barnabas. God works through the likes of you and me. God works in the margins.

Do you believe that? Do you experience that?

For Meditation This Day

God, help me hear the voices and see the witness of your new beginnings in my own life, in the lives of those around me.

WEEK TWO

Renunciation

Biblical spirituality involves the discipline of renouncing old ways. Though sometimes lost in the maze of setting aside minor pastimes, this discipline is called to mind during Lent in the "giving up" of some aspect of one's routine life. But the roots go far deeper. Repentance invokes the biblical sanction of renunciation. In Colossians 3, Paul writes of those things that must be "put to death" and "gotten rid of" before we turn to the list of qualities with which we are to put on or "clothe" ourselves. New life and beginnings come at the cost of renunciation.

Day 1

DINAH

The Cycle of Violence

GENESIS 34:1-31

*"Simeon and Levi are brothers; weapons of violence
are their swords....Cursed be their anger."*

—Genesis 49:5, 7

NE OF THIS generation's chief learnings in the field of domestic abuse has been the cyclical nature of its violence. Part of the cycle has to do with the pattern in which a buildup of tension leads to a violent outburst, followed by a "honeymoon" period; then tensions build again. Another understanding of the cycle has to do with the escalation of violence over time. Violence is never satisfied to remain at one level of intensity. Violence begets greater violence.

Dinah's story begins with an act of violence. While visiting other women in the region, a man of wealth and power named Shechem rapes Dinah. (Shechem is the name both of the prince and of the city in which he lives.) His act does violence to the code of hospitality, even as he does violence to the body and spirit of this young woman.

At this point, the story takes an awkward turn—awkward, at least, to modern sensibilities. The narrator depicts a change of heart by Shechem toward Dinah: love and tenderness now describe his disposition toward her. Shechem requests that his father make it possible for him to wed his victim. And therein resides the awkwardness. Is Shechem merely in a stage of infatuation or even denial that his initial act was one of violence? Once he possesses her, will violence return to the relationship? Such concerns, though valid from a modern perspective, are not those of the text. The story proceeds as if Shechem is sincere and as if the cycle of violence is as old as the hills.

A parley takes place: Shechem and his father Hamor on one side, the aggrieved sons of Jacob (and brothers of Dinah) on the other. Father and son plead for Dinah to be given in marriage at any cost. The brothers respond by doing violence to the truth of their intentions. They set a high cost for their sister's wedding: the circumcision of every male in the city of Shechem. Circumcision serves as a powerful vehicle for their deceit. It had been given to Abraham as the sign of the covenant (Gen. 17:9-14), the sign of belonging to God and to God's community. Now it becomes the means to wreak vengeance on the deceived.

While the men of Shechem are still in pain from the physical procedure involved in circumcision, two brothers of Dinah sneak into the city and kill not only Shechem and Hamor but all the other males. The other brothers follow, plundering and looting the city, taking the wives and children as captives.

The breaking of hospitality and the rape of Dinah beget the telling of lies, and the twisting of religious ritual begets the slaughter of a city. Violence cycles throughout this story. And even then, it does not stop. It recycles to twist and disrupt the gift of family. Father berates sons—not so much for the horridness of their act, but because they "brought trouble on me" (34:30). Sons respond with a rhetorical question, "Should our sister be treated like a whore?" (34:31), a question that totally ignores the disproportion of their action in comparison to the original offense.

Without knowing, both father and sons capture the essence of the evil of violence. It elevates self, it ignores proportion, and it generates only destruction. Shechem, Hamor, and all their kinsmen lie dead. Widows and orphans abound. Family divides

against itself, a division Jacob will reflect in his dying words
(49:5-7).

And Dinah: Whatever happened to Dinah in all this?

For Meditation This Day

Against whom would I rather lash out than be reconciled? God,
renew within me your forgiveness, that I may risk forgiving.

Day 2

DINAH

Missing in Action

GENESIS 34:1-31

O God, do not keep silence; do not hold your peace.
—Psalm 83:1

N READING through the story of Dinah a second
time, did you note a curious fact? The text preserves
no word or action, no thought or emotion of Dinah.
Though the entire narrative revolves around her, Dinah does not
act in the drama: she is only acted upon. Dinah is the victim *par
excellence*, stripped of all identity beyond what is done to or
because of her.

Dinah is not alone in that regard in this episode. As the violence ripples outward from Shechem's act to the brothers' vengeance, who gets swept away? Not simply Shechem, the
instigator; not only Hamor, the negotiator for a settlement on marriage and reconciliation among peoples—a host of anonymous

innocents are also made victims. No names are given the men of Shechem who perish. No faces are attached to the little ones of the city who are carried away. No characters are connected to the widows who are "made their prey" (34:29). Violence strips away all notion of personhood, so it may act without the restraint of respect for others. Violence recognizes only self: self-interest, self-protection, self-justification.

But there is one more character whom violence seeks to make a missing victim in this narrative. No word or action, no thought or emotion attaches to God in this entire chapter. The text offers no reference to God's presence, as if the stripping away of personhood in the process of doing violence involves the stripping away of God's presence.

Innocent victims of violence such as Dinah bring the question of God's presence to the fore. Where was God in the rape? Where was God in the deceitful promotion of circumcision? Where was God when Simeon and Levi and the others swung swords and plunged knives and made prey of innocents? Genesis 34 does us a favor by not rushing to provide saccharine answers. Its silence concerning God forces us to ponder the question for ourselves. And the question is by no means limited to the violence done to this young woman and the people of Shechem. Where is God today when children kill children? Where is God today when persons who have vowed to love and cherish become batterers and abusers? Where is God today when...?

In *Night*, a book written by Auschwitz survivor Elie Wiesel, the issue of God's absence in the face of violence finds stark witness in a disturbing passage. The SS hangs two Jewish men and a youth in front of the whole camp. The men die quickly, but the death throes of the youth last for half an hour.

"Where is God? Where is He?" someone behind me asked....For more than half an hour [the youth] stayed there, struggling between life and death, dying in slow agony under our eyes....Behind me I heard the same man asking: "Where is God now?" And I heard a voice within me answer him: "Where is He? Here He is—He is hanging here on this gallows" (1960, 61–62).

Where is God to be found in the face of violence? Among the victims—with Dinah, with the populace of Shechem, with the innocents and missing ones created in every age by those who wield force and do violence, who wreak havoc and destroy.

In Genesis 34 violence holds the day, muting God's voice and influence. But Genesis 34 is not the final word. If Wiesel is right and God is to be found among the victims, another word looms. Matthew records a parable whose core affirms that our treatment of the least among us mirrors our treatment of God (Matt. 25:31–46). And who can deny that those whom violence robs of human dignity and personal identity number among the least?

The God of Dinah is the God who will give her what her brothers and even the text withhold: her own words and actions, her own thoughts and emotions...her own missing life. The God of Dinah is the God who will judge the perpetrators of violence by their treatment of the least. Doing violence belongs to the age that is passing away, to old ways in need of renouncing.

For Meditation This Day

Turn me, O God, from the ways of violence, violence wrought by hand or word or attitude. Turn me...and through me, turn us.

Day 3

HAMAN

The Roots of Hatred

ESTHER 2:5; 3:1-13

All who hate a brother or sister are murderers.
—1 John 3:15

HAT PERSON can give eyewitness testimony to the first time in history when light-skinned and dark-skinned peoples experienced hatred toward one another? Who among the elders of Dublin and Belfast can remember the exact moment when Irish Protestants and Catholics first felt enmity for one another?

The answer, of course, is no one. Hatred possesses the peculiar ability to be remembered beyond any specific memory, certainly beyond the scope of any one lifetime. One can be raised in its prejudice and loathing much the same way one learns language as an infant and child. Hatred is simply there: in the background and between the lines, waiting for a spark to trigger it.

Such an understanding illuminates the abrupt transformation of Haman from elevated official of King Ahasuerus to planner of history's first pogrom (persecution unto death) of the Jews. Mordecai, a Jewish official in the king's court, does not bow down to Haman because of his Judaism (3:2, 4). As the king has ordered that such deference be shown, Mordecai clearly commits an act of civil disobedience. But how does Haman move from an affront by one person to the proposed destruction of an entire people (3:6)?

"Haman son of Hammedatha the *Agagite*" (3:1, *italics added*).

We sometimes gloss over genealogical details in biblical works; and in so doing, we often miss extraordinary insights the author provides. The detail of "Agagite" does not merely trace a family tree; it traces the coursing of a blood feud. The Amalekites were Israel's most hated enemies, going back to the time of the Exodus (Exod. 17:14; Deut. 25:17-19). Agag, an Amalekite king during the reign of Saul (1 Sam. 15:8-33), had warred against Saul, a member of the Benjaminite tribe whose father's name was Kish. And how does Esther introduce Mordecai?—"son of Jair son of Shimei son of *Kish*, a *Benjaminite*" (2:5, *italics added*).

More than six hundred years have passed since Mordecai's and Haman's royal ancestors fought and perhaps another two or three hundred years more since Haman's progenitors attacked those of Mordecai in the wilderness. But Haman takes up the feud and the hatred as if he had stood among the desert raiders and alongside the fallen Agag. With hatred, past merges and future disappears in present opportunities for revenge. Even as time blurs, so does all sense of proportion. Mordecai's singular refusal to bow translates into Haman's justification for genocide.

Hatred, however, seldom finds the courage to act alone; it recruits others to do the work. Haman thinks it beneath him to confront Mordecai (3:6), much less the whole Jewish people. So Haman enlists the king with charges of how different these people are (3:8). Deviation from the norm is no modern invention in the enlistment of hatred's coworkers nor is the promise of a payoff (3:9). Haman funds the enterprise with the literally incredible offer of ten thousand talents (two-thirds of the annual income of the entire empire).

So run the roots of hatred in the story of Haman, roots that survive with different names and histories to this day. We ignore Haman at our own risk, not simply in the "wide-angle" replays of this story where genocide is not far from the truth in hatred's modern political and racial incarnations. We ignore Haman at our own risk when we fail to trace the roots of hatred in our lives. Those roots still can emerge from times and events long past to shape how we view and treat others, especially those we deem different.

For Meditation This Day

Where do I feel hatred's seduction? Upon whom do I look down just because they differ from me? Deliver me, O God, from hatred.

Day 4

HAMAN

The Fruits of Hatred

ESTHER 5:9-14; 7:1-10

Better is a dinner of vegetables where love is
than a fatted ox and hatred with it.
—Proverbs 15:17

THE ADAGE OF sowing the wind only to reap the whirlwind finds disastrous example in the outcome of Haman's hatred. The "firstfruits" of hatred with Haman (or anyone else) come in the dual blossom of self-absorption and obsession with the hated. In the first of the texts from Esther, Mordecai's continued refusal to pay Haman homage disrupts an otherwise pleasant day. The refusal infuriates Haman. Yet how does he respond? He calls together friends and family and begins a litany of self-importance: "Haman recounted to them the splendor of his riches, the number of his sons, all the promotions" (5:11). When confronted by the one person he seems unable to impress or control, Haman engages in the equivalent of a child's "neener-neener-neener." Look what I've got! Look who I am! Look at me!

Hatred results in extraordinarily childish but by no means innocent behavior. Every affirmation of what he has and who he is only leads Haman one step closer to the realization that Mordecai is not moved. And hatred, true hatred, cannot abide being ignored by the object of its disdain. So in the midst of recalling all that he has, Haman pouts. All of this is nothing so long as Mordecai is around. The obsession is complete. For life to continue, hatred demands annihilation of the hated.

How might one respond to hatred? The most demanding choice would require unmasking hatred's folly before the one who clings to it. No one confronts Haman in that manner. No one suggests a middle ground of cooling off hatred's fire by soothing Haman's spirit with the assurance that Mordecai is just one harmless Jew who'll soon be dead. Instead, even as hatred initially recruited others to do its work, now hatred finds a supportive chorus from its well-wishers. Erect a gallows for Mordecai, they urge. Standing in the way of hatred is risky business, lest one become the new object of loathing. "Go along to get along" marks their advice.

Another fruit of hatred is blindness to reality, and in the end Haman victimizes himself. The queen whose favor he boasts turns out to be the niece of Mordecai, a Jewess who risks pleading for her people before the king. Haman cannot foresee that the end he has plotted for Mordecai and his people turns into the sentence carried out against him and his followers. "So they hanged Haman on the gallows that he had prepared for Mordecai.…So the Jews struck down all their enemies with the sword, slaughtering, and destroying them, and did as they pleased to those who hated them" (7:10; 9:5).

The dramatic reversal recounted in Esther is not a morality lesson against the exercise of violence; it is a testimony to the ends of hatred. One cannot build a life on hatred without falling prey to it. Hatred, like violence, is not content to remain on one level. Hatred against Mordecai leads to hatred against an entire people. Hatred that simmers inside a person's spirit—or a society's mind-set—works like acid, not glue. It consumes self in the absorption with self. It loses sight of others in its obsession with the enemy. The Aryan Nations Church or other such groups serve as grotesque examples of hatred's way among us. One need not call for genocide or race war to suffer its consequences. One need only to hate and to let hatred fester.

For Meditation This Day

"Those who say, 'I love God,' and hate their brothers or sisters, are liars" (1 John 4:20). God of love, save me from the lie whose name is hate.

Day 5

SIMON MAGUS

Gimmicks and Gospel

ACTS 8:9-13

Then the devil took him to Jerusalem,
and placed him on the pinnacle of the temple,
saying to him, "If you are the Son of God,
throw yourself down from here."

—Luke 4:9

N THE EARLY 1980s, a church near the one I served publicized a youth meeting with an odd twist. The youth pastor would be swallowing goldfish. I did not attend, though perhaps I should have. Then I could have verified my assumption that once a crowd was gathered and the "trick" was over, the gospel would be preached to amazed teens. The question is, What sort of gospel would it have been? Would it have been a gospel that relied on gimmicks to get attention, since crosses and calls to service were not all that inviting? And if interest began to wane, what would be done next to hold the attention of those hooked by martyred goldfish—stuff telephone booths for Jesus?

Tricks and tricksters offer shortcuts to gathering crowds and getting attention. My friends at the other church will argue persuasively that the imperative of reaching as many people as possible with the message of Jesus Christ warrants leeway in getting them to listen. The end justifies the means. I worry that the means also tend to color the ends. People lured with gimmicks may consider the gimmicks as part of the gospel.

[47]

Simon understands what catches people's eyes and holds their attention: He wows them with magic. Indeed, he comes to be known as Simon Magus (the Latin root for "magic"). Today's reading affirms his allure when it declares not once but twice that Simon amazes the people. But perhaps most telling of all in these opening verses is the link between amazement and listening: "And they listened eagerly to him because for a long time he had amazed them with his magic" (8:11). Simon keeps the crowd and becomes a celebrity because he puts on a good show.

But shows and celebrities do not disciples make. Amazement and faith are not synonyms. The problem with gimmicks and the celebrities they create is the question of encores. How many rabbits can be pulled out of a hat before the audience begins to yawn and look for a new act? Simon finds himself usurped by the preaching—not the parlor tricks—of Philip. Those enraptured by the Magician's sleight of hand become a discipled community by the Deacon's baptizing hands. (For Philip's identity as deacon, see Acts 6:2-5). The crowd exchanges listening for following.

As today's reading winds down, Simon believes and undergoes baptism. And most intriguing, Simon "stayed constantly with Philip and was amazed when he saw the signs and great miracles that took place" (8:13). Simon Magus, who wowed the crowds, is now himself the wowed. As is true elsewhere in Acts, physical manifestations of wonder accompany the preaching of God's kingdom and Jesus. Signs and miracles are the currency in which Simon has long traded. But what does one make of the fact that the author of Acts links the belief of the crowds with gospel proclamation and the belief of Simon with amazement at signs and miracles?

The story of Simon is not yet over, so the answer waits. But even at this early juncture, these verses raise a warning flag. Producing amazement is not identical to producing belief. Christian witness is not a "whatever gets people's attention" nor even a "whatever works" proposition. Evangelism demands integrity between the word presented and the means of presentation. Gospel gimmicks may be a contradiction in terms.

For Meditation This Day

What and whom do we allow to grab our attention and catch our ears? Help us to listen for you, O Christ, and in listening, to follow.

Day 6

SIMON MAGUS

Everything Has a Price

ACTS 8:18-24

"Be on your guard against all kinds of greed."
—Luke 12:15

N OLD CHILDREN'S story counsels that "gimmes never get." Greed, however, is not a struggle limited to childhood. Always wanting what another has plagues more than a few adults. And the wanting only grows worse when money enters the picture, not merely as the object desired but more so as a final word as to how all the cravings may be secured. Certainly commercials confirm the idea that if you have enough money (or line of credit), the world is yours.

Simon Magus does not have media public relations campaigns to excuse or to condition his yearning. What he does have is the experience—or memory—of power. "This man is the *power* of God that is called Great" (8:10, *italics added*). Simon has both wielded and been recognized as power. But now the crowd turns elsewhere—first to Philip and then to Peter and John. Simon turns in that direction himself—but whether out of sincere faith or sheer amazement, we are left to judge. As if to tip the scales of that judgment, Simon yearns to wield power again so much that he offers money for the power of bestowing the Holy Spirit (8:18-19). Simon is a very modern individual. He understands that everything has a price—and Simon is willing to pay his own way.

However, the gospel is not a consumer product in disguise. In words that rival Jesus' scathing condemnation of religious hypocrites as whitewashed tombs (Matt. 23:27, 33), Peter censures Simon in harsh terms. At the core of the denunciation is Simon's heart: not right, ill-intended for having thought it possible to purchase God's gift. Peter invokes repentance and prayer on Simon's part for the sake of forgiveness.

Simon answers by saying, "Pray for me" (8:24). That is well and good, but does Simon pray for himself? Does Simon engage in the hard work of repentance and prayer or merely seek Peter to do it for him? His previous conduct suggests that such a strategy would not be inconsistent. Rather than take on the path of self-emptying discipleship that provides no guarantee of privilege or power, Simon has attempted a shortcut to power by putting cash on the barrel to get what he wants now. And using money to get what we want differs little, if any, from using people for the same end. "Give me also this power" and "Pray for me" may well be two sides of the same coin.

To this day "simony" describes the sin of attempting to purchase church office or authority. Perhaps we are no longer so crass as Simon in terms of paying for spiritual favors. But greed remains a powerful factor in the lives of individuals and institutions—including the church. Whether the accumulation consists of wealth or power or status is inconsequential. Whenever we elevate self-aggrandizement above all else, avarice figures into the equation.

Peter offers part of the warning: "I see that you are in the gall of bitterness and the chains of wickedness" (8:23). Peter takes greed seriously because of its seductive binding of the human spirit. Acts does not mention Simon Magus again, but in the writings of the early church, he becomes a figure of exceptional controversy. Legends about him abound. Eusebius, a Christian theologian of the late third century, goes so far as to call Simon the father of all heresy.

Merited or not, the charge cannot be proved. The connection between one so associated with heresy and one so associated with greed is interesting. In greed's reduction of God's spirit to a commodity, God is put up for sale...and that may be the greatest heresy of all.

For Meditation This Day

Keep me, O God, from greed's dulling of conscience, cheapening of life, and subjugating of spirit to self.

Day 7

MAKING CONNECTIONS

*Put to death, therefore, whatever
in you is earthly.*
—Colossians 3:5

HE VOICES SPEAKING from the margins in this week's readings are not the sort we like to hear. Their stories are not easy; their messages are not comfortable. And, to our dismay, their soundings in our lives may strike us as far too familiar. But we neglect these voices to our own detriment, for they identify with unsettling accuracy old ways in need of renouncing even today.

The voice of Dinah, muted by her repeated victimization, still emerges from between the lines to speak poignantly and powerfully about the necessity of breaking with violence as a means of redress. Her story clearly demonstrates that reliance on violence guarantees further brutality, with an ever-widening circle of innocents caught up in its wake. The way Dinah's silence mirrors the absence of God in this story underscores the peril we invite by acting indifferently to any sense of God's presence. We remove all restraints once we exorcise God from the scene and stand accountable only to self. But God will not always remain in the wings, a certainty that stands as both hope for the innocent and judgment for the violent.

The voice of Haman cries out the folly of a life consumed by hatred. When read in narrative form from an objective distance, the story seems unreal. Then again, Holocaust and ethnic cleansing seem unreal if kept at a distance. But hatred never works at a distance. It scours the human heart of compassion and love in hope of transforming the enemy into a mere object or crude caricature. And in that scouring of the heart, hatred puts its practitioners at greatest risk. "Those who say, 'I love God,' and hate their brothers or sisters, are liars" (1 John 4:20). Hatred and grace do not coexist. Those who do not renounce the way of hate, like Haman, become its prey.

In the voice of Simon Magus, we hear a clear warning against the influence of greed. Neither ministry nor Spirit is for sale to the highest bidder, a point to keep in mind when generous offers or dire warnings accompany the church's blessing of this position or that candidate. Simon's request focused on the seeking of power, and the church does well to recall that power in the community of Jesus involves not privileged position but sacrificial servanthood (Mark 10:41-45). The renunciation evoked by Simon's story runs against the grain of the way things typically work in a market- and power-driven world. Possessions and privilege are not stepping-stones to faith; and unless kept in perspective, they can become its obstacles.

All these voices remind us of hard words spoken by Jesus. I suspect we prefer the gospel's tender and gracious side—of lambs brought back from harm's way and prodigals received. But we sometimes ignore or underplay the side of Jesus' ministry that seeks our conversion rather than our comfort. Nowhere do we see that ministry more clearly than in Jesus' journey to Jerusalem, a journey the church revisits each Lent. Renunciation marks the way, and words of that journey issue calls to cross-taking and self-denying. Those calls confront old ways in need of turning or rejecting, if the grace of new life and fresh starts is to take root and find room to grow.

Biblical spirituality involves the discipline of renunciation. In the voices of Dinah, Haman, and Simon Magus, we hear the consequences of old ways not being set aside but clasped tightly. Even in the margins, the consequences of violence and hatred and greed cost dearly. May we listen closely to these voices that we may take seriously the ways that drag us down and hold us back from God, from one another, from our very selves.

For Meditation This Day

God, tune my ear to listen to the harder words of grace, that in listening I might turn—and be turned—from old to new.

WEEK THREE

∽

Trust

Biblical spirituality invites trust of God with gracious abandon. Such trust wholeheartedly and unreservedly places self and destiny in God's hands. Such trust enables persons to move beyond circumstances that might otherwise create despair or fear to a spirit of hope and confident reliance. On the eve of death when Jesus prays "not my will but yours be done" (Luke 22:42), Jesus trusts God with gracious abandon. We trust God with gracious abandon in Lent when we look upon crosses and see not the finality of death's power but the witness to life's hope.

Day 1

HANNAH

Taking the Leap

1 SAMUEL 1:1-18

Out of the depths I cry to you, O Lord.
—Psalm 130:1

 HEN DID YOU last cry to God out of the depths? In the wake of a loved one's death...in the midst of an embittered estrangement...in the pain of illness or disease...in your own doubting of God's goodness, triggered by some terrible event?

Sometimes the church does a disservice by leaving the impression that lament or protest represents bad faith on our part and, therefore, does not belong in our prayers or devotions or corporate worship. It's better to purse our lips, suffer in silence, and keep our questions—not to mention anger—to ourselves.

But God knows the human heart from the inside. Flight from God, physical or spiritual, is folly (Psalm 139:7-12). Seeking God with what resides deep within us coupled with the depths into which we have fallen provides the difficult but redemptive course. We act in trust when we bring before God the whole of our lives, not just what we think would please (or at least not offend) God.

When Hannah presents herself before the Lord at the shrine in Shiloh, she comes weighed down with extraordinary baggage. In a culture that views fertility as God's blessing, Hannah remains barren. To exacerbate the situation, her husband's other wife Peninnah not only has sons and daughters, but Peninnah "used to provoke [Hannah] severely, to irritate her, because the Lord had closed her womb" (1:6).

Hannah prays to God in *deep distress*, a Hebrew phrase that the King James Version renders as "bitterness of soul." One might assume that bitterness would counsel Hannah against prayer, waiting until her feelings are less severe. Or one might presume bitterness would only lash out against God. After all, the text does intimate twice (1:5, 6) that God stands as the cause for Hannah's barrenness.

Without masking her bitterness (the text adds that she "wept bitterly"), Hannah prays—in and of itself a remarkable act of trust. Yet the substance of her prayer may exceed even her act of faith in praying. For Hannah accompanies her prayer for a child with a pledge to return the child to God as a nazirite, one consecrated to God. Hannah entrusts herself to God, the source of life. If that trust issues in a child, Hannah vows to entrust that gift of life back into God's hands and purposes.

Does Hannah understand what she promises and what its keeping will entail? We will touch on such issues in the next day's reading. For now it is enough to contemplate in awe the trust revealed in Hannah's vow.

The testing of her trust does not take long. The priest Eli, charged with oversight of the Shiloh shrine, misunderstands her. Not hearing the words, he takes her mouthing of a silent prayer as evidence of drunkenness. Hannah, as in her prayer to God, does not hide her distress from Eli. Without disclosing the particulars, she declares she has been "pouring out my soul before the Lord." Eli's benediction that God grant her petition closes the encounter with the hope that Hannah will be heard.

Does the disappearance of Hannah's sadness in verse 18 come from the confidence aroused by Eli's affirmation or from the emotional release of pouring out her soul in prayer or from the calm generated by her trusting enough in God to pray—or do all three explanations really point to the same core truth? Out of bitterness, out of the very depth of her spirit and situation, Hannah takes a leap of faith: She trusts God.

For Meditation This Day

God, when I feel I cannot possibly pray, help me to pray. When it seems I cannot possibly trust, help me to trust—in you.

Day 2

HANNAH

Keeping the Trust
1 SAMUEL 1:19-28

Surely God is my salvation; I will trust.
—Isaiah 12:2

N 1505 the twenty-one-year-old son of a copper miner found himself caught outdoors in a thunderstorm. The young man vowed that if God delivered him from the storm, he would change his life's plans and become a monk. Friends, and especially his father, counseled him against keeping the vow. The youth himself later wrote that he initially regretted making it. But two weeks after the storm, Martin Luther entered the Augustinian monastery at Erfurt.

Perhaps similar doubts arise in Hannah's mind and heart when she swells with life for the first time. In her crisis of childlessness, a time of raw emotions evidenced by her distress and weeping (1:10), Hannah has promised to give her firstborn to God. Promises often fly freely in the heat of the moment. Given Hannah's duress, one might find cause to excuse her from the vow. Who would expect a mother to hand over a child? What kind of God would enforce such a vow?

But the story, amazingly, centers not on revelation about the character of God but about the character of Hannah. Even after Hannah has cradled and nursed this child in her arms, even after the God-given son has received her love and care—even then, Hannah keeps her vow. With accompanying sacrifices that must have seemed extraordinarily meager when compared to the toddler beside her, Hannah hands Samuel over to Eli and leaves. A parent cannot read the story of Hannah with detachment. Put yourself in her place; put your child in Samuel's place…if you can. If you dare.

What makes her act possible? The same thing that made her original prayer possible: trust, radical trust in God. In bringing Samuel to Eli, Hannah trusts God absolutely with the care and keeping of her beloved son. In a sense the story parallels Abraham's near-sacrifice of Isaac. The chief difference is that Abraham returned home with a child, while Hannah walks home alone—but not in despair. Hannah walks home in trust. She walks in the trust that God will care for her son in her absence. "She left him there *for the Lord* " (1:28, *italics added*).

Hannah trusts God with gracious abandon. The abandonment relates not to how she acts toward her son but how she responds to her own prerogatives as mother and parent. Hannah leaves Samuel at Shiloh, not because of personal doubts about her abilities as a mother but out of sheer trust in God. The graciousness of Hannah's act derives from God's gift of grace in bringing life to a barren woman, just as grace evidences itself in Hannah's promise keeping. Who would require Hannah to give over her only child? Who would blame her for withholding him from such a vow? Yet, just as God remembers her and gives Samuel, Hannah remembers her vow and returns Samuel.

Sometimes trust in God becomes an innocuous byword among us, reduced to a motto stamped on coins. As Hannah's voice reveals, trust in God promotes the most selfless of actions when truly enacted and stamped on the heart. Likewise Hannah's example challenges us to consider the depth of our own trust in God. Do we trust God so deeply that we could entrust what (and whom) we hold dearest to God's care rather than our own? Perhaps Hannah speaks to Jesus' later words on discipleship, words that also presume a radical trust in God: "For those who want to save their life will lose it, and those who lose their life for my sake, and for the sake of the gospel, will save it" (Mark 8:35).

May we learn trust at Hannah's side in order to prepare for our walk at Jesus' side.

For Meditation This Day

All I have and am comes from you, O God, so teach me to trust all I have and all I am to you.

Day 3

THE CENTURION

By Word of Mouth

LUKE 7:1-6

*The Lord God has given me the tongue of a teacher,
that I may know how to sustain the weary
with a word.*

—Isaiah 50:4

OULD YOU TRUST something or someone known to you only by word of mouth? It depends. If you have a cough and a friend tells you about a folk remedy she heard about, you might give it a try without much thought. On the other hand, if you have been diagnosed with terminal cancer, and a friend tells you about some exotic (and costly) treatment overseas—what would you do then? You might seek additional information: some written documentation, a conversation with another patient who has undergone the therapy, a heart-to-heart visit with your physician, or all of the above. We find it difficult to trust word-of-mouth information when the stakes are high and life is on the line.

So what do we make of this Roman centurion in Luke? We do not know his name. We know he has a gravely ill servant whom he holds in high regard. And we know, from the testimony of the Jewish elders he dispatches to Jesus, that this centurion has treated his Jewish neighbors in Capernaum with generosity. Luke reports they go so far as to say, "He *loves* our people" (7:5, *italics added*). Luke here uses the Greek word *agape*: the self-giving love commanded by Jesus for neighbor (Mark 12:31) and enemy (Matt. 5:44) as well as for other followers (John 13:34). The centurion does innately what Jesus seeks from those who would be his disciples.

The centurion's request catches our interest even more than his beneficent neighborliness. Facing a favored servant's impending death, the centurion engages in a risky act of trust. "When he heard about Jesus, he sent some Jewish elders to him, asking him to come and heal his slave" (7:3). This unnamed centurion has not met Jesus. He has not had opportunity to question the rabbi about the means of his miraculous healings. All the centurion has is word-of-mouth information. And remember that the line separating word of mouth from rumor and gossip is rarely clear. Yet, having only heard of Jesus, he sends for Jesus to come and heal. The centurion trusts the rabbi to help.

What makes this man's trust more remarkable is what little we know of his identity. He is a centurion and in all probability a Gentile (7:6). Animosity already smolders between the Roman occupation forces and the Jewish inhabitants of Galilee and Judea, animosity that will burst into open revolt in less than a generation. But here a centurion seeks the help of a rabbi. A Gentile seeks the ministrations of a Jew. The normal state of distrust between Jews and Gentiles finds contradiction in the centurion's trust. Such trust is not without risk. What would his subordinates and commanders think of a centurion who dabbles in the superstitions of the Jews by calling on one of their healers?

What the centurion stands to lose within his military community does not compare to what he stands to lose without Jesus' intervention: the life of a valued servant. As a result the centurion abandons the conventional wisdom of keeping the worlds of Gentile and Jew separate for the sake of trusting one of whom he has only heard. The centurion's trust is as remarkable as it is transforming. Sight unseen, he relies on Jesus.

Sight unseen, by word of mouth. That is basically what we have to go on too. Like the centurion, we have heard of Jesus. Like the centurion, will we trust in Jesus?

For Meditation This Day

"Blessed are those who have not seen and yet have come to believe." May you still bless faith that takes you at your word, O God.

Day 4

THE CENTURION

By Word Alone
LUKE 7:6-10

By faith we understand that the worlds were prepared by the word of God.
—Hebrews 11:3

THE NOTION OF "by word alone" is less an article of faith these days than a stretch of the imagination. For example, we have grown accustomed—or is it acquiescent—to the breaking of words issued in political campaigns. Those who believe the promises and naturally expect the keeping of those politically motivated pledges are dismissed as naive unsophisticates who are out of touch with the demands of "linguistic fluidity" in political campaigns. Those who trust in words alone are apt to find themselves grasping a handful of air. Did not Jesus teach that actions matter more than words, even right words (Matt. 21:28–32)? Yes…but!

But what? "By faith we understand that the worlds were prepared by the word" (Heb. 11:3). "In the beginning was the Word" (John 1:1). Creation and redemption find their origin, if we trust these texts, in a word—a word whose speaking spins worlds into being and love into incarnation, a word whose power awaits human trust to unleash its redeeming and creative possibilities.

The centurion of Luke 7 has trusted in Jesus solely on the basis of words he has heard. Now in the extraordinary turn his story takes, the centurion declares he stands ready to trust the word of Jesus alone to heal his stricken servant: "Only speak the word and let my servant be healed" (7:7).

"Only speak the word." In Book Six (*The Magician's Nephew*) of the Christian fantasy The Chronicles of Narnia by C. S. Lewis, creation occurs when Aslan the lion begins to sing. As he sings, things happen. Where there had been only darkness, stars explode into light, a sun ascends, and hills rise. The song changes, and animals spring from the earth. Lewis's fable portrays life summoned by a song—a word. That image bears close resemblance to the biblical account in Genesis 1. Each day of creation proceeds, and each work of creation follows at the speaking of God's word: "Let there be…." God speaks, and by word alone creation lives.

"Only speak the word." The centurion certainly knows nothing of C. S. Lewis. He probably knows little if anything of the Hebrew story of beginnings. But the centurion does understand the power and authority of word. "For I also am a man set under authority" (7:8). In that understanding, he trusts the power of word alone to heal, to bring life. The response to such "word alone" trust amazes Jesus (7:9). Only one other time do the Gospels recount Jesus' amazement, and then it is at the unbelief he encounters in his hometown of Nazareth among fellow Jews (Mark 6:6). But here the faith of a Gentile centurion amazes Jesus.

The centurion's faith may still rightly amaze us. Why? The centurion's story reminds us that trusting in words alone—and Word alone—is not a fool's errand. Jesus' word heals the servant. The story of the centurion reminds us that the cynicism of our age directed toward words alone need not infect our faith. Jesus' word proves trustworthy. In hope of a word, the centurion trusts. And in that trust, the centurion is not disappointed.

Word and words remain at the core of faith. The trust conveyed in the centurion's "only speak the word" challenges our willingness to trust in the power of words alone and Word alone to heal and redeem and create new life in our midst. The Word spoken—in worship, in prayer, in scripture, in service, in community life—awaits our trust. "Only speak the word."

For Meditation This Day

God who speaks, grant me ears to hear and heart to trust the word you speak, the word you enflesh, the word you promise in Jesus Christ.

Day 5

STEPHEN

A Full Life

ACTS 6:1-15

May the God of hope fill you with all joy and peace in believing, so that
you may abound in hope by the power of the Holy Spirit.

—Romans 15:13

N ADVERTISING CAMPAIGN for a credit card company relates the price of various items, implicitly made attainable by use of the card, whose purchase leads to a priceless experience. The purchase of greens fees and golf equipment results in a hole in one. The purchase of a formal gown, opera glasses, and season tickets makes possible a series of evenings with one's spouse. The clear message is this: If you don't spend money for the stuff, you won't have an opportunity to enjoy the priceless experience. A full life, in the theology of the ad campaign, involves acquiring material stepping-stones to happiness. Do you believe that? Or, more to the purpose of the advertising campaign designers, do you buy that?

If not, how do you define a "full" life? Mourners and pastors employ that phrase with some frequency in the context of funerals or celebration of life services. Sometimes a "full" life in those settings becomes little more than a euphemism for the advanced age of the deceased. The problem is that the accumulation of many years, like the accumulation of many things, does not a full life make. A full life has far more to do with the person's experiences and how those experiences have shaped and revealed—and bequeathed—character.

Stephen provides a striking character study for a life that is full. Not once, not twice, but three times today's text from Acts asserts qualities that fill his life. When the time comes for the community to select seven deacons, the apostles advise the choice of those "full of the Spirit and of wisdom" (6:3). Stephen heads that list, which includes the description of him as "full of faith and the Holy Spirit" (6:5). Later the preface to Stephen's ministry reads, "Stephen, full of grace and power" (6:8).

Wisdom and faith, grace and power—such gifts of Spirit and qualities of character fill Stephen's life. These are not items for sale on the marketplace for those blessed with platinum credit ratings, as the story of Simon Magus warned. These are not the inevitable consequences of old age, as if years alone bestow such endowments. Wisdom and faith, grace and power come to Stephen as they would come to any of us. They are gifts of God whose formation combines personal nurture with Spirit's leading.

That these gifts reside in Stephen becomes apparent in the community's choice of Stephen as one of the seven. That Stephen continues to exercise these gifts finds witness in his ensuing ministry (6:8)—a ministry, interestingly enough, that leads to opposition, conflict, and judgment (6:9-14). A full life is not typically associated with discord. A full life, one might think, would enjoy its gifts in calm and peace. But wisdom and faith, grace and power do not insure tranquility. Stephen's full life leads, if not drives, him into ministry and conflict.

So whose version of the full life do we prefer for ourselves and our churches—the version where fullness has for its ultimate goal our satiation and ease, regardless of price; or the version where fullness has for its underlying purpose our service, often accompanied by struggle? Stephen, full of wisdom, faith, grace, and power, trusted God enough to risk fullness of life in service. To what end do we trust God with what fills our lives?

For Meditation This Day

You fill my life in so many ways. Help me see those gifts rightly, O God, and move me to use them freely in your service.

Day 6

STEPHEN

Christlike

ACTS 7:54-60

And it was in Antioch that the disciples were first called "Christians."

—Acts 11:26

N SEVERAL VERSIONS of the Afro-American spiritual "Lord, I Want to Be a Christian," the final verse invokes this prayer: "Lord, I want to be like Jesus." I want to be like Jesus. "Be careful what you pray for, lest you receive it" may serve as a fair caution here. Being like Jesus involves acting like Jesus, and the boulevard shared by Lord and disciple goes by the name of Calvary.

Stephen, full of wisdom and faith, full of grace and power, stands as one whose life now fills with danger and vulnerability. His accusers bring him to the Sanhedrin and charge Stephen, like Jesus, with prophesying against the Temple (Acts 6:14; see also Matt. 26:61). Stephen ignores the specific charges against him, choosing to respond in the form of a sermon. He traces Israel's history through patriarchs and Exodus, concluding with a powerful counteraccusation against the council leaders for their role in the betrayal and death of the Righteous One (Acts 7:52).

Today's reading resumes the story of Stephen at this point; Stephen's trust of God confronts the face of death, the ultimate test of any trust. Also at this point, Stephen's trust of God unfolds in a series of actions that mirror Jesus' acts in suffering and dying.

The crowd rages against Stephen. Instead of seeing the hatred surrounding him, however, Stephen trusts the hope before him. Filled with the Holy Spirit (fullness of life marks Stephen even at the brink of death), Stephen sees the heavens open and the Son of Man standing beside God (7:56). This vision parallels Jesus' words to the high priest at his trial (Matt. 26:64). Just as those words evoked the clamor for Jesus' death, so now does Stephen's vision trigger his martyrdom.

Two final actions link Stephen with Jesus. First he offers a prayer: "Lord Jesus, receive my spirit" (7:59). During the normal course of our days, trust in God tends to result from (and be aimed at) God's keeping our lives intact. Death can create a crisis of seeming abandonment by God. Stephen might have succumbed to such a spirit, crying out against a God who leaves him to his enemies. Yet Stephen trusts God, yielding his life into God's hands. We can trust life's giver, despite the claims of those who take God's prerogative into their own hands by taking life.

Stephen's second, and dying, action comes in his response to those who rain down stones upon his head and body: "Lord, do not hold this sin against them" (7:60; see also Luke 23:34).

One cannot offer such words without the most radical trust in God. This trust does not ask God to wreak vengeance on enemies because of what they have done to us. This trust asks that God redeem them in spite of what they have done to us. To trust God with the forgiveness of one's enemies—for Stephen and Jesus—graciously abandons revenge for mercy.

"Lord, I want to be like Jesus." Do I? Do I want to be like

Jesus, so my eyes can still see cause for hope when everyone around sees only reason to hate? Do I want to be like Jesus, so when prayers for deliverance do not remove cups of suffering I can still trust God? Do I want to be like Jesus, so I can pray God's forgiveness for those who cause me pain and a cross?

Christlike, Stephen lives and dies. With Stephen, may we want to be like Jesus. From Stephen, may we learn to trust like Jesus.

For Meditation This Day

O God, make my trust in you my hope in life, my grace for others, my peace within myself.

Day 7
MAKING CONNECTIONS

Trust in the Lord, and do good.
—Psalm 37:3

THE VOICES IN this past week's stories share two things in common. All three speak of radical trust in God, and all three arise from the periphery of the predominant mainstream of each character's culture. Hannah's story begins in the context of barrenness, a state viewed with disdain and theological judgment by her contemporaries. The centurion stands as Gentile and oppressor for most Jews, both symbols of what ailed first-century Palestine. Stephen stands condemned by the duly constituted authorities of Temple and Torah, judged a transgressor against his day's religious establishment. Perhaps the trust of these persons might simply be a "what have I got to lose" desperation. Yet they had everything to lose by such trust.

Hannah stood to lose what little remained of her respect by daring to trust that God would heed the prayer of one who was barren. Her voice challenges the way we dismiss people deemed unworthy of God's attention, much less grace, because of how or who we judge them to be. What seems so clear to our eyes, as to Peninnah's, may actually blind us to God's working in the margins. When Hannah's prayer is heard and a child comes, the stakes of trust become astronomical in her keeping the vow to give the child to God. Trust, in light of Hannah's example, finds expression not in what we cling to in life but what we entrust into God's hands. Such trust lets go but does not lose. For nothing and no one are lost when given to God.

The centurion risks the loss of his authority by relying on the word of one supposedly subject to him. The centurion's voice confronts our ease in condemning what (and whom) we find alien to the normal circles in which we live and move and find our definitions of the world and God affirmed. In such places we typically trust only those who have proved their mettle to us. When the centurion summons Jesus after only hearing of him, and later when he dispatches the message of "only speak the word," we see the possibility of a far more radical trust at work— trust that abandons personal authority for the sake of another's life, trust that comes down to reliance on a holy presence brought only through word.

Stephen's trust risks the condemnation of those whom culture recognizes as God's spokespersons. What does it mean for someone to entrust his or her life to God, when others who claim to act in the name of God condemn that life? When the stones cease flying and Stephen lies bloodied and dead, and the authorities return to positions of power, who determines victory? Trust that abandons life itself into the hands of God cannot be reckoned by executioners left standing at the end of such a day. Stephen's voice bears witness that vindication of trust in God may well wait for times and circumstances beyond our sight, beyond our control—when trust truly must trust.

Such voices make clear that trust is a profound element of spiritual discipline, pushing us to consider how deeply our trust of God runs. As such, these voices parallel the story—and stories—of Jesus. Hannah trusts God so deeply as to offer her firstborn to God's service. Jesus' very incarnation in one sense represents God's trusting in a love for creation so deeply as to offer the only Begotten for creation's redeeming. Trust—for God, for Hannah—withholds nothing.

Jesus frequently called persons to demonstrate similar trust: fishers to give up nets, all they had known, for the uncertainties of following; a rich young ruler to give up wealth, all that assured him of life's blessing, to seek after life's eternal nature. Calling others to trust, however, involves providing the example. Gethsemane's "not my will but yours be done" provides one such moment. Calvary provides the climax. There we see trust graciously abandoning all, even life, into God's hands.

Biblical spirituality invites us to trust God with abandon. In the actions of Hannah and the centurion and Stephen, we see the possibility of such trust in extreme circumstances. And in the passion of Jesus Christ, we see the trust of God put to the test by being put to the cross...and still, trust triumphs. "Into your hands I commend my spirit."

Into God's hands may we entrust our whole lives.

For Meditation This Day

Gracious God, receive my life to use as you will, to grace as you please, to love as only you may. I trust you with my life.

WEEK FOUR

❧

Courage

Biblical spirituality inspires acts of courage born of commitment to God. Such courage does not call persons to do the impossible but faithfully and selflessly to do what they can when they could have chosen otherwise. Lent recalls the courage of Jesus who "set his face to go to Jerusalem" (Luke 9:51), in spite of understanding what awaited him there. Jesus' example invokes courage today as you and I translate words of commitment to God into freely chosen actions that place others above self—and God above all, for trust of God opens the door to courage.

Day 1

SHIPHRAH
PUAH

Obedience and Courage
EXODUS 1:8-17

"Choose this day whom you will serve."
—Joshua 24:15

N OCTOBER 1945 the International Military Tribunal convened in the German city of Nürnberg for the purpose of trying Nazi war criminals. Political leaders, military officers, and industrialists comprised the bulk of those charged with, among other things, crimes against humanity. Those proceedings set the precedent that "following orders" could not be claimed as an excuse for engaging in such crimes. However, Nazi Germany does not stand as the first example where governmental edict provoked a crisis for persons ordered to carry out inhuman policy.

Changing times have fallen on the Israelites in Egypt. A new Pharaoh comes to power, to whom the name of Joseph means nothing. From Pharaoh's ignorance of Joseph and his kin arises the fear of what the Hebrews might do. From Pharaoh's fear comes repression in the form of slave labor. From repression comes an ultimate solution to the dilemma caused by Pharaoh's order to kill all newborn Hebrew males. From ignorance to fear to repression to death: It is a descent not unknown in our time. And the choice confronting Shiphrah and Puah recounts this descent.

The very anonymity of these two women provides an unlikely counterweight to Pharaoh's power. Exodus provides no word of their ancestry, nor does the text hint at any characteristics or qualities that would set them apart for what is about to unfold. They are two ordinary Hebrew women, whose only point of intersection with the likes of Pharaoh comes through their vocation of midwifery. Pharaoh, in contrast, stands as the very incarnation of divinity in that day's culture. He speaks with the authority of state and of a god. The living deity orders the two midwives to carry out his policy of eradication: You have a job to do. Do it!

The Hebrew word for midwife literally means "to help to bear." Therein lies the dilemma. Shiphrah and Puah's vocation requires that they help bear life; their mandate is to end life. The story sets the stage for a decision that will risk either their calling or their obedience. Risk is always a prerequisite for courage. "The midwives feared God; they did not do as the king of Egypt commanded them, but they let the boys live" (1:17).

Shiphrah and Puah make a critical and dangerous distinction. Despite all appearances to the contrary, they choose to act as though Pharaoh is not the highest authority in the land. They recognize a higher claim in the God of Abraham and Isaac and Jacob. The moral and ethical demands of this God override the temporal authority of Pharaoh, even in the land of Egypt. This God demands not only right worship but right action. Shiphrah and Puah's obedience takes the form of disobedience. Following orders becomes secondary to following God. Others live because of their courage.

Courage is not what a person risks when there is no other choice. Courage risks self-jeopardizing action when other—and less risky—options abound. Shiphrah and Puah could have shrugged shoulders and sighed, "What could we do? It was

Pharaoh's command." But they chose not to. Courage does not belong to the brave but to the faithful. Courage arises in the most ordinary of persons who, in a single moment of decision, act in a way that puts self aside for the sake of others. Courage invokes obedience to God that supersedes—and risks—the claims of human authority.

From the margins of Pharaoh's land, with no traits that otherwise set them apart, Shiphrah and Puah act with courage.

For Meditation This Day

Encourage me, O God, to keep faith with you and to act for others.

Day 2

SHIPHRAH

PUAH

Why?

EXODUS 1:18-22

"For I will give you words and a wisdom that none of your opponents will be able to withstand or contradict."

—Luke 21:15

 N THE 1960s, "situation ethics" came into vogue— and passed out of popularity almost as quickly. Its basic Christian expression argued that the uniqueness of each life situation requires a response tailored to what love would demand in that particular instance. The weaknesses of individualistic interpretations and the lack of a clearly defined center beyond a vague notion of "love" led to a rapid fall into disfavor. Disfavor, however, does not constitute absolute disavowal. The ongoing courage of Shiphrah and Puah before Pharaoh sets a startling precedent of situational ethics.

Pharaoh apparently has received reports that the killing of Hebrew male newborns is not proceeding as ordered. He summons the midwives to ask the obvious—and potentially fatal—question of why. We might expect the midwives to engage in a heroic act of confrontive truth-telling: We serve God, not you; what you order is immoral and impossible for us to follow in good conscience. Instead, Shiphrah and Puah respond by telling Pharaoh that the problem arises because the Hebrew mothers give birth before they arrive.

One might wonder where Shiphrah and Puah's courage has gone. With their lives on the line, do they now back down and make excuses in order to protect their own skins? However you read their response in verse 19, Shiphrah and Puah lie to Pharaoh. They assess the situation and make truth a victim. Why? What motivates their resorting to falsehood?

If Shiphrah and Puah speak plainly, two things will likely happen. First, the two women will suffer death for deliberate disobedience of Pharaoh. Second, Pharaoh will put others in their place to do his original bidding. In their assessment of the situation and in the ensuing lie, we may hear and see another act of courage on their part. They dare to deceive Pharaoh, buying more time to spare more children. Shiphrah and Puah risk the good of truth for a greater good—life. And what is more important here: that Pharaoh be told this wrong or that additional children be given reprieve? Which would you choose? Which would you consider more courageous?

Life can present situations where choices are not so much between good and evil as between which of two goods is more pressing. In the cross of Jesus Christ, the good pleasure of God with the Beloved (Luke 3:22) becomes subordinate to the good pleasure of God with creation (Luke 2:15). God risks the Beloved in favor of redemption. Why? "For God so loved the world...."

As the story of Shiphrah and Puah draws to a close, courage reveals not only its rewards but its limits. On the reward side, God blesses the two midwives with families (1:21). On the limit side, Pharaoh assigns not two midwives but "all his people" (1:22) the task of killing the Hebrew male infants. Shiphrah and Puah can save no more. So at the end of the story, have Shiphrah and Puah failed? No. They did all they could—and that too is part of the meaning of courage. You do not have to do the inconceivable, only what is within your capacity.

The courage of Shiphrah and Puah puts self at risk for faithfulness to God. The courage of Shiphrah and Puah even puts truth at risk for the greater good of saving innocents. Shiphrah and Puah risk courage for the sake of new life. So may we.

For Meditation This Day

God of the future, give us courage for this day: courage to trust your presence, courage to still our fears, courage to seek new life.

Day 3

NATHAN

The Power of Word and Story

2 SAMUEL 12:1-6

Indeed, the word of God is living and active,
sharper than any two-edged sword.
—Hebrews 4:12

 YOUNG BOY OF nine or ten surveyed the counters in a neighborhood drugstore. The intended target had been the trays of candies and gum, but the salesclerk seemed never to stray far from them. The boy had already summoned the nerve to leave the store with something stolen, when an alternative came to mind. With stealth and cunning, the boy slipped a roll of transparent tape into one pocket and strolled out, triumphant. After dinner, the boy sat on a sidewalk step in the front yard with his father.

The elder raised neither hand nor voice. Word alone conveyed disappointment and discipline and hopes for better choices.

I never shoplifted again.

Words possess remarkable potential and power to heal, to indict, to forgive, to love. You would not be reading this book if you did not believe in the power of words. And the forming of words into story raises the level of that potential and power. The Bible would not have endured over the centuries unless persons and communities of faith found the potential of its storied word to convey God's presence and purposes. Of all his teachings, it is Jesus' use of parable—story—that is most distinctive...and, some would say, most persuasive.

Second Samuel 11 tells the sordid story of David's treachery toward Uriah in order to possess Bathsheba. How long had Nathan lived with the details of this story: the seduction, the loyalty of Uriah, the plot to ensure Uriah's death, the marriage, the child? Does God, in sending Nathan to David, also send the prophet his story? Or does the story emerge from Nathan's heart? If so, the prophet might well have been a bard. In any event, Nathan conveys God's displeasure (2 Sam. 11:27) by telling David a story.

Everybody likes a story. And when Nathan begins by saying, "There were two men in a certain city..." (12:1), David can relax. The story is not about him. It's about these other two people. Nathan sets David up to listen, ears and spirit wide open, because for David this is not so much hearing as overhearing. The words, the story, involve someone else. Right?

Nathan's story entices David into the middle of its starkly defined tale of greed and innocence. It would not have been unusual for the king to be called on to mediate some dispute between persons in his realm. But the story Nathan tells invokes no middle ground from its listener. The oppression, the theft, the abuse: All are way out of balance, way out of justice. By story's end, David the dispassionate hearer has become David the avenging angel. Story alone generates David's anger, an anger that demands restitution at best and death at worst. Nathan's story moves the one who acted with absolutely no pity toward Uriah to condemn this rich man "because he had no pity" (12:6).

The power of story invites us deeply into the narrative, where we are confronted with the truth about ourselves. Truth, whether its accompanying details be related in factual or fictional form, stands at the core of story. Nathan displays courage by crafting words into a story aimed at confronting a king with truth. What stories tell the truth *about* you, tell the truth *to* you? "A young boy of nine or ten surveyed the counters...." So one such story began for me.

For Meditation This Day

God whose word is life: help me hear, help me heed the stories that tell the truth of my life.

Day 4

NATHAN

Afflicting the Comfortable

2 SAMUEL 12:7-15

"Now I have put my words in your mouth...to destroy
and to overthrow, to build and to plant."
—Jeremiah 1:9, 10

URTON BROWN SERVED as one of my mentors in the pastorate. I recall an installation service at which Burton gave the so-called "charge" to the new minister: a combination pep talk, advisory session, and traditional questions posed to the installee. The questions proceeded rather normally, including the one about promising to comfort the afflicted in the parish. But then Burton paused for a moment, looked at the young minister before him, and asked, "And will you also afflict the comfortable?" Laughter broke out in the congregation—some I suspect, fueled by the recognition that Burton's question was far more than a play on words. At times, "afflicting the comfortable" defines precisely what ministry (and courage) requires.

Nathan's confrontation of David begins with a masterful story. By its end David rails against the rich man devoid of pity. But the story remains one of "two men in a certain city," not David and Uriah. At this point, Nathan might have seized the temptation to tread lightly in drawing parallels between the story and David's life: "I want you to think about this story, and your life in the past year, and get back to me when you think you understand." Was David not the one to whom God had earlier declared the promise of establishing his kingdom and throne forever (2 Sam. 7:16)? Did Samuel not affirm that God's rejection of Saul for David was tied to God's seeking "a man after [God's] own heart" (1 Sam. 13:14)? Is the truth spoken so boldly to one so favored and "positioned"?

"Nathan said to David, 'You are the man!'" (12:7). In Nathan courage speaks truth to power. Courage afflicts the comfortable. Courage changes the story from third-person objective to second-person accusative: You are the man! And courage relates the consequences of David's treachery (12:10-15).

The text relates the terse summary that Nathan, having spoken, went home. No delight follows from bearing this word to David. Courage does and says what it must and goes its way. Courage is its own reward, and its own burden.

Let us not misunderstand the narrative. This story does not make into a universal virtue the troubling of the comfortable or the powerful in life for the mere sake of troubling them. Nathan's reproach is not a blanket condemnation of power or David's holding of it. Nathan indicts David's abuse of those powers in the injustice he commanded.

In Jesus' ministry, no disciple rivaled the position given to Simon Peter: the rock upon whom Jesus said he would build his church, the one in whose hands Jesus would entrust the keys of the kingdom (Matt. 16:18-19). Yet when Peter rejects Jesus' teaching of a suffering and dying Christ, Jesus responds with one of the gospel's harshest words to disciple or foe: "Get behind me, Satan! You are a stumbling block to me" (16:23). Jesus' courage afflicted Peter's cozy theology where Messiah always triumphs and crosses never appear with truthfulness about Jerusalem, discipleship, and the way life is truly saved.

When Burton Brown charged that young pastor with afflicting the comfortable, he invoked the same truthfulness that Nathan and Jesus exercised. Keep that in mind and heart not only when God seeks you to speak such truth, but when God calls you to listen...and hear the truth afflicting you.

For Meditation This Day

Holy God, if you would afflict me with your truth, then do so; only let your grace encourage me all the more.

Day 5

THE MAN BORN BLIND

Opened—and Affirming

JOHN 9:1-23

For in [Christ] every one of God's promises is a "Yes."
—2 Corinthians 1:20

THE STORY IS told of Michelangelo's visiting a marble quarry in search of sculpting material. The quarry master naturally took great pains to point out the slabs and blocks of surpassing beauty. Michelangelo's selecting an obviously flawed piece took him aback. When the quarry master could not persuade him to choose otherwise, he asked the sculptor why he insisted on this one. "Because," Michelangelo said, "there is an angel inside waiting to be set free."

Jesus' disciples see a man blind from birth. Their eyes see only a problem, only cause for blame: "Who sinned, this man or his parents, that he was born blind?" (John 9:2). In Jesus' eyes, the sight (and person) before him is not a study in guilt but an opportunity for God's works (9:3): an angel struggling to emerge from behind a stone-solid veil. The means to do that work seem uncomfortably common: spittle, dirt, touch, word. Yet when all merge in action, healing comes. The man born blind emerges with eyes opened. Can you imagine seeing colors for the first time? Can you imagine seeing the texture of human flesh for the first time? The opening is not just of eyes but of life.

Unlike Mark, in whose Gospel wondrous things happen and the narrative abruptly moves on, John describes miracles that linger on into discussion and misunderstanding, into controversy and pronouncement. The unnamed man whose eyes—and with it, life—have been opened scarcely has time to take in the sights before he finds himself immersed in questions: "How were your eyes opened...where is he...what do you say about him?" (1:10, 12, 17).

Interrogation belongs to the crowd and then to officials offended by a Sabbath healing. But affirmations in this narrative come from two persons. Jesus makes the first affirmation. When Jesus touches the blind man and sends him to the pool to wash, he affirms this man as valued of God. By acknowledging this man to be somebody beyond an exercise in finger-pointing, Jesus opens him to life. The courage on Jesus' part relates to this healing's taking place on a Sabbath, duly noted in the debate his action triggers.

But courage also belongs to the second person who makes affirmations in this story. When some question the recipient's identity, as if to lessen the import of Jesus' miracle, the man born blind speaks: "I am the man" (9:9). When others of authority question Jesus' character and seek the newly sighted one's opinion, the man born blind affirms, "He is a prophet" (9:17). Perhaps he has not possessed sight long enough to know how to read what others expect him to say. Or perhaps he simply possesses the courage to say things as he now sees them.

In any case, the man born blind, the man whose life has been opened by Jesus, makes two key affirmations: I am the man; he is a prophet. I am the one who never saw a face before this day, the one others rarely saw without speculating who was to blame for me. I am that one. And he is a prophet, who does not so much foretell the future as open it, who heals one such as I. I can say who he is because I know who I was—and now am.

To be opened by God marks the gift of grace; to be affirming of God displays the gratitude for grace: for the man born blind, for you, for me…for everyone God in Christ opens to life.

For Meditation This Day

When you affirm me as your child, O God, you open me to your grace. So give me courage to affirm who I am, and who you are.

Day 6

THE MAN BORN BLIND

Topsy-Turvy

JOHN 9:24-41

The wolf shall live with the lamb,
the leopard shall lie down with the kid,
…and a little child shall lead them.

—Isaiah 11:6

ONG BEFORE science-fiction films and series toyed with the idea of parallel universes inhabited by our opposites, Lewis Carroll wrote of a young girl who tumbled into the backwards land behind a looking glass. In the contrary nature of that place, the denizens celebrated unbirthdays, and a word only meant "just what I choose it to mean." *Topsy-turvy* might describe such a place or state of relationships where all is upside-down from what we might expect.

Topsy-turvy calls to mind the reversal of status quo inherent in today's reading. For a second time the religious authorities call in the man born blind for interrogation. They confront him with their knowledge of Jesus' sin, perhaps a continuing reference to their scornful view of Jesus' Sabbath-breaking.

The man responds with ignorance of Jesus' sin and testimony of his own changed status at Jesus' hands ("though I was blind, now I see"[9:25]—a line echoed in the familiar text of "Amazing Grace").

But now topsy-turvy enters the text. When pressed about Jesus' actions, the man born blind questions the authorities' intent by asking if they want to become Jesus' disciples (John 9:27). When they then spout theology as a safe haven for their skepticism about Jesus, the man rejoins with an even deeper theological argument, challenging skepticism with faith: "If this man were not from God, he could do nothing" (9:33). Stop here. A man born blind had no access to the scrolls long studied by his antagonists. A man born blind might well have been considered unclean, therefore unable to enter the Temple. Yet here a man born blind outpoints the theologians in theology. It is a world turned upside down.

And it is an uncomfortably modern world that does not tolerate persons' speaking out of their delegated place. "You were born entirely in sins, and are you trying to teach us?" (9:34). The author of John's Gospel often states the truth ironically on the lips of Jesus' opponents (or misunderstanding disciples). As Jesus revealed at the beginning of this story, the authorities are dead wrong about this man's origin in sin. Their presumption of his trying to teach them, however, is dead right. They simply do not see that he does. Thus follow Jesus' concluding words at chapter's end: "Now that you say, 'We see,' your sin remains" (9:41).

In a world turned upside down, it takes courage to speak the truth, for truth in topsy-turvy may seem like falsehood. The man born blind demonstrates courage in speaking truth about Jesus to those whose minds have settled the matter already. As the story comes into focus, they seek not testimony but corroboration of their own truth.

Perhaps we should not be too harsh on these folks. How do we react to news that challenges our well-settled views of the world—particularly of persons for whom we have no use? When our hearts and institutions already "know" who is the sinner, do we attend words and stories that come from the margins and seem incredible? "Never since the world began has it been heard that anyone opened the eyes of a person born blind" (9:32). For some these words are proof enough that such a miracle can't happen: This man must be a liar and Jesus a sinner. Of course, never since the world began has it been heard that anyone raised someone from the dead. The gospel not only presumes but proclaims a world turned topsy-turvy—and a God who does the turning.

For Meditation This Day

O God, grant me courage to live as if your kingdom comes, as if your Christ lives, as if you love me. And grant me courage to trust you with the "as ifs."

Day 7

MAKING
CONNECTIONS

Do not fear, for I have redeemed you;
I have called you by name,
you are mine.

—Isaiah 43:1

TWO PREVARICATORS, one storyteller, and a man with mud still streaking his face who presumes to teach teachers without ever having laid eyes on a book: our first choices for learning the spiritual discipline of courage, right? Yet from their incredibly diverse voices, we hear the testimony to courage emerging in choices made and commitments kept.

Shiphrah and Puah begin the parade. They reveal the way in which common persons may suddenly and unwillfully be thrust into critical moments of decision. Courage in such situations need not take extravagant or superhuman form. Their story insists that courage may come in as simple a thing as remaining true to our vocation or identity when powerful forces persuade us to be (or do) other than who we are. Integrity looms large in courage. Unsettlingly the story of Shiphrah and Puah also makes real the dilemma faced when courage finds itself having to choose between the greater of two goods. How do we decide? The midwives' fear of God is their bottom-line commitment. What is ours?

Nathan courageously confronts an erring king, yet he does so with a story that David may easily misunderstand. The courage of Nathan the storyteller reveals the courage to trust in the power of words to invite empathy as preparation for "you are the man!" But it is easy to grow impatient with words, particularly when injustice holds court. Taking matters into our own hands by way of retaliation or vengeance in kind seduces as strongly today as in David's time, whether in cutthroat business deals or terrorist reprisals—or antiterrorist overkills. Courage, however, does not swagger. It simply and profoundly speaks truth to power. It sets the power of words to work in the human heart and mind.

The man born blind refuses to be silent. He does not know when to be still, even when folks who clearly convey they are his betters shush him. He cannot speak other than who he is and what Jesus has done. That is courage, then and now. It takes courage to speak what you know to be true through experience when society and persons of power would convince you otherwise. It takes courage to say God loves Palestinians when standing next to an ultra-orthodox synagogue in Tel Aviv. It takes courage to say God loves Israelis when you own a shop in the Gaza Strip. Courage, then and now, involves risk. Courage risks the possibility of change—the possibility that, for once, the eyes of one born blind may be opened. And if one, why not others?

From these surprising characters who speak from the margins of the biblical narrative, not to mention the margins of their own society, it is not difficult to see Jesus' profile. Attending to the voice of Shiphrah and Puah, we recall the courage of Jesus who will not be tempted from his vocation as a suffering Messiah—not by Satan in the wilderness, not by Peter at his side. Listening to the voice of Nathan, we remember the courage of Jesus who confronts armed opponents in Gethsemane's garden with words but not sword. Discerning the voice of the one born blind, we give thanks for the courage of Jesus to speak truth to Pilate and to a thief crucified beside him.

Biblical spirituality evokes acts of courage. The midwives, the prophet, the sighted one: All share in common with Jesus the courage that derives from devotion to God. May their example and faith encourage us!

For Meditation This Day

Holy Presence, in crisis and in quiet, in the deep waters or standing on high ground: Be with me, and give me your courage. In Jesus Christ.

WEEK FIVE

~

Servanthood

Biblical spirituality engages in service rooted in love. Service without love differs little from uncaring drudgery. Love provides the invigorating motive of willing self-investment. Love without service fails the test of embodiment. Such love merits the condemnation levied in James on those who pray for another's well-being without accompanying action (James 2:15). On the outskirts of Jerusalem with its impending suffering, Jesus commands servanthood (Matt. 20:20-28). Calvary confirms the depth of love enacted by the One who not only commanded service but came to serve.

Day 1

BARUCH

Behind the Scenes
JEREMIAH 36:1-4

*"Beware of practicing your piety before others
in order to be seen by them."*
—Matthew 6:1

AVE YOU EVER watched the entire line of credits following a movie? The cast of actors generally leads off the scrolling with size of name sometimes a telling barometer of contract and/or ego. By far, however, the greatest number of acknowledgments goes to those who never appear on screen. These persons labor, contribute, and provide support "behind the scenes," out of sight from camera and audience.

Those who work "behind the scenes" are by no means limited to the theatrical world. In any setting where human beings gather to accomplish something, we will find—or quickly discover the need for—those who carry on their business out of sight and fanfare. For those few who achieve the designation of greatness, countless others have contributed mightily to that achievement without its accompanying fame.

Baruch does not likely roll off your tongue with trademark familiarity. Certainly he does not carry with him the recognition of, say, a Jeremiah. Yet without Baruch, Jeremiah's voice would be silent. Baruch served as Jeremiah's scribe.

In Baruch's time, the art of writing was just that, an art whose practitioners were few and far between. But despite their highly marketable skill, scribes did not stand at the forefront of affairs. A scribe's reputation depended not on originality or creativity but on the ability to duplicate the thoughts and words of others. Scribes then do not correspond to our conception of a writer today, someone with a distinctive voice or style or "niche." Scribes served as human dictation machines for others in the spotlight—kings, business persons...or prophets.

"Then Jeremiah called Baruch son of Neriah, and Baruch wrote on a scroll at Jeremiah's dictation all the words of the Lord that he had spoken to him" (36:4). This is not glamorous work that requires extraordinary creativity of thought. It is one letter, one word at a time. Meticulously keeping the lines straight, Baruch's hands move the stylus. Ears concentrate on Jeremiah's voice, slowed enough not to race ahead of scribe yet paced to keep sense and narrative flowing.

If you think scribal work grand and exciting, ask a friend to read Jeremiah 1 aloud while you write the words in longhand on a blank sheet of paper. Write clearly enough for others to read your writing. Carefully record every word exactly as said. On completion, prepare to write another fifty-one chapters. Then you may understand Baruch's service. Actually you would need to take one more step. Even though the writing would be in your hand, you would have to tell others that these are not your words at all. The words and the name belong to another. You would remain behind the scenes. No one reads on Sunday, "a lesson from Jeremiah as dictated to Baruch."

Baruch's story probably resembles our own. Most of us expend more of our service in the background than the spotlight. Behind-the-scenes servants rarely get rounds of applause, whether ladling soup for homeless folk or doing the legwork for the stewardship committee. To many eyes, "behind the scenes" remains there—but not for God. In the opening passage quoted from Matthew, Jesus goes on to identify God as the One who sees in secret, the One who sees behind the scenes and sees those who render service there for the pure love of it.

For Meditation This Day

God, may my service to you and others not depend on the notoriety it brings. Rather, may it thrive in expressing my love for you.

Day 2

BARUCH

Sharing the Risks
JEREMIAH 36:5-32

"'Servants are not greater than their master.' If they
persecuted me, they will persecute you."
—John 15:20

 N 1215, the Fourth Lateran Council of Western Christianity addressed the "problem" of unconverted Jewry by decreeing that Jews must wear some form of distinctive dress or identifying mark on their clothing. Over the centuries, this practice experienced periodic revivals when anti-Semitism waxed strong. The most commonly recognized and enduring symbol aimed at separating Jews from their neighbors was the yellow star. The yellow star became one of Nazi Germany's earliest strategies for isolating the Jews, a prelude to the violent persecutions and "final solution" that would follow. The edict of wearing a yellow star carried into the nations that Germany conquered and occupied.

The plan misfired in Denmark. In September 1943 German occupation authorities there decided the time had come to address "the Jewish problem." King Christian X sent a terse message to Berlin: "We have no Jewish problem. We have only Danes." The refusal of Danish Christians to separate themselves from Danish Jews still lives on in the legend of the king's wearing the yellow star on his morning ride through the streets of Copenhagen, joined by thousands of Danes. What is not legend but fact is that by late 1943, Gentile Danes had smuggled over 7,000 Danish Jews to Sweden, with less than 500 captured. The citizens of Denmark placed themselves in harm's way for the sake of their Jewish citizens, and by doing so saved most of them.

Imagine now the scene our text depicts. Baruch, having finally completed the task of recording Jeremiah's words, busies himself with putting away the unused scroll and styluses, capping the containers of ink for another day. His job is done. Or is it? "By the way," Jeremiah intones, "since I am banned from the Temple, I need you to go there and read everything you've just written to all of the people of Judah." Hmmmm.

Baruch, as required by his profession, is an educated man. Surely he knows the confrontational import of Jeremiah's words, as Jeremiah himself suggests by "the anger and wrath that the Lord has pronounced against this people" (36:7). The safer option would involve telling Jeremiah that "I am a writer, not a prophet." Who could blame Baruch for doing his job of scribing and no more? Servanthood, however, does not consist of "just doing a job" and then moving on to safer ground when trouble shows. "Baruch son of Neriah did all that the prophet Jeremiah ordered him" (36:8). Baruch's supportive role goes beyond the letter of Jeremiah's dictation. Servanthood shares the risk.

As the narrative unfolds, the risk proves genuine. Royal officials, alarmed at the message, request a command performance by Baruch (36:11-15). At its conclusion, having ascertained the scribe's role, they warn Baruch not just to tell Jeremiah to hide but to hide himself as well. This apprehension proves valid once the royal officials read the scroll to King Jehoiakim. First slicing the scroll into strips, Jehoiakim burns the scraps until nothing remains. His parting command orders the arrest of Baruch and Jeremiah.

Days and weeks of painstaking work are lost. Prophet and secretary have gone into hiding. So does Baruch finally separate himself from Jeremiah, not daring to associate ever again with one who has brought such trouble upon him? Read Jeremiah 36:32. Baruch not only rewrites all the words on the first scroll at Jeremiah's dictation but others as well. Why do this, since the king remains angry? The answer: The word has been given to Jeremiah by God (36:27), and Baruch remains a willing servant both of Jeremiah and that word.

Baruch willingly shares the risk of serving God by refusing to separate himself from Jeremiah, though we rarely hear this scribe's name. The people of Denmark, whose names are largely forgotten, willingly shared the risk of serving God by refusing to separate themselves from their Jewish neighbors. So it is with us. Servanthood willingly shares the risk of doing God's work, even when it comes unaccompanied by the accolades of fame.

For Meditation This Day

God, grant me to serve you faithfully, whether that service serves me well or not.

Day 3

THE WOMAN WHO ANOINTS

Servanthood Embodied

LUKE 7:36-47

Do not neglect to show hospitality to strangers, for by doing that some have entertained angels without knowing it.

—Hebrews 13:2

Y FIRST PARISH was nestled in the far northeast corner of the state of Washington. A U.S. Customs port on the border with British Columbia served as the next stop north. To the east a rough U. S. Forest Service road wound over a pass before finding its way to a small settlement in Idaho. Given the isolation, the church uncannily received more than its share of transients seeking food or shelter. Where they were headed and why did not always make sense. But the church responded. Some folks in the church, and probably more in the wider community, questioned such aid to transients. Were we really helping them, or just enabling bad choices? Were we encouraging others to put the touch on us as word spread?

Quite possibly Bonnie would have been at the forefront of such objections. She and Gene had worked hard to make a nice home for themselves and for the five children they raised. What they got they earned. Yet Bonnie was the one who told my wife that when someone asked for food or help, she was not there to judge. She was there to pack the bag of groceries or make the sandwiches or get the gas tank filled. And when Bonnie spoke of why she was there, she also affirmed why the church was there. Servanthood comes in the doing, not just the talking—especially when its actions are subject to misinterpretation.

Jesus had reclined (7:36) at Simon's table already, an indication that this event took more the form of a banquet than an ordinary meal. A large gathering, others besides the Pharisee and rabbi may have crowded table and room—making it possible for an unnamed woman to come in the door and to the table unchallenged. Unnamed but not unknown. The narrator depicts her as "a woman in the city, who was a sinner" (7:37), an assessment Simon later shares (7:39). Some have identified her sin as prostitution, though the text gives no precise answer. Perhaps that association comes in what appears to be her highly sensual contact with Jesus. Her tears bathe his feet, which she then dries with her hair before anointing them with oil (7:38).

Simon sees in her actions a flaw in Jesus' "prophethood." Jesus sees in her actions a flaw in Simon's servanthood. "I entered your house; you gave me no water...you gave me no kiss...you did not anoint" (7:44-46). The woman who is a sinner provides the hospitality, the servanthood, that Simon the (righteous) Pharisee neglects. Simon opens his table to Jesus, an admirable act of association. Yet Simon's hospitality to Jesus remains somewhat on the surface, at arm's length; whereas the woman *touches* Jesus (7:39). The very intimacy that Simon condemns on her part becomes the embodiment of servanthood, servanthood that Jesus commends as having "shown great love" (7:47).

Servanthood requires embodiment. Jesus' upbraiding of Simon for inaction implies that this woman touches a need overlooked by the host. Simon's behavior is akin to sending money to a person or group in crisis without ever having or seeking contact with the ones in distress. The woman who anoints Jesus does not hand him the alabaster jar and say, "Enjoy." Her tears wash, her hair dries, her lips kiss, her hands anoint. She embodies servant-hood as her life touches Jesus with love.

For Meditation This Day

Servant God, whom would you have me touch? For whom shall I risk misunderstood actions for the sake of rendering service that shows great love?

Day 4

THE WOMAN WHO ANOINTS

Forgiveness and Love

LUKE 7:47–50

And now faith, hope, and love abide, these three;
and the greatest of these is love.
—1 Corinthians 13:13

HAT LITTLE I knew of the late Governor George Wallace, I did not like: his defiant stand in front of the University of Alabama to block the enrollment of black students, the blatant racism of his public rhetoric. An assassin's bullet in 1972 left him paralyzed, unable to continue his aggressive political agenda. A curious thing happened over the years. Word leaked out of a change in heart, a sincere regret for his earlier alliance with the forces of race hatred. Based on my early images of Governor Wallace, I always thought he had a lot for which he needed forgiveness. Apparently forgiveness came, and its coming changed him. My last image of him involves a number of African-American mourners at his funeral. I wonder if the presence of those African Americans stemmed from knowing they had lost someone who came, albeit late, to love them?

The idea seems odd, especially given Governor Wallace's early days. Yet the idea meshes with what we learn from Jesus about the link between forgiveness and love and the woman who anoints him. "Her sins, which were many, have been forgiven; hence she has shown great love" (7:47). In the mathematics of grace, explicit in this declaration and implicit in the parable that prepares it (7:41-43), forgiveness and love come in direct proportion. The greater the forgiveness, Jesus asserts, the greater the love.

Jesus does not cast this woman in some idealized aura, as if her love demonstrates that she really wasn't that bad a person to begin with. *Many* is the adjective Jesus employs to describe her sins…and he leaves it at that. Jesus does not dwell on the nature or depravity of her sin, forcing her to relive a past she longs to set aside. In truth, forgiveness has come to her already ("have been forgiven," 7:47), even before Jesus pronounces his word of forgiveness in verse 48. Jesus says that the proof of her forgiveness comes in her showing great love.

Now there is a novel idea for the church, not to mention society. What do we seek or insist upon as evidence of forgiveness? Must we recite the right words of contrition or continually confess Jesus' deliverance in language that meets the theological criteria of liberals or evangelicals or charismatics? Must we grovel appropriately (and for a time determined by others)? The woman who anoints Jesus shows great love—and that, apparently, is all that Jesus needs to know. Love forms the intended outcome of forgiveness, then and now.

In the example of the woman who anoints Jesus, that truth confronts us square in the face—and heart. The service this woman renders, in acts of love, forms the sign and seal of her forgiveness. Love even forms the sign and seal of her salvation, if we take Jesus' closing benediction at face value: "Your faith has saved you; go in peace" (7:50). The woman's faith? Where has this woman showed faith? She has not even spoken! Where is her creed? "She stood behind him at his feet, weeping, and began to bathe his feet" (7:38). Her creed speaks in her deed; her faith comes in her love. She tends to the most humble act of service for the one who then pronounces her not only forgiven but saved. Love flows from forgiveness and is its best evidence.

How deeply will you love? In the light and story of this woman, Jesus pronounces, as deeply as you have been forgiven.

For Meditation This Day

Help me know the depth of your mercy and grace for my life, O God, that I might rightly know how to love.

Day 5

PHOEBE

A Benefactor of Many

ROMANS 16:1-2

"For where your treasure is, there your heart will be also."
—Matthew 6:21

 SMALL GROUP GATHERED in a living room to discuss a church's troubled finances. Stewardship came to the fore in the challenge of two poorer families' sacrificial levels of giving that did not mirror patterns in the congregation. Some countered with the argument that money reflected only one aspect of church support and did not serve as an accurate indicator of commitment. A mediating pastor from the wider church interjected that Jesus once hinted at just such a link, quoting the verse above from Matthew. One of the gatekeepers of that congregation replied, "Then Jesus and I disagree."

Paul commends a woman called Phoebe to the church at Rome because, among other things, she has been a *benefactor. Benefactor,* a word whose literal meaning in Greek is "one who stands before," only occurs in the New Testament in this one text. Its meaning (and Phoebe's example of it) thus retains a degree of mystery. Its corresponding word in Latin is *patron,* someone who saw to the financial support of an individual, group, or cause. Some people suggest that the term might even have referred to the support rendered by a citizen to obtain the freedom of a slave—a process that involved the payment of a fee.

The specifics of Phoebe's "benefactoring" we do not know. Regarding the truth of her providing for others, Paul among them, the text leaves no doubt. Phoebe's life and wealth benefited and supported the lives of others. Even her Christian service took the form of a benefactor.

The text implicitly connects Phoebe as benefactor with Phoebe as Christian servant. Paul declares her a deacon (*diakonos*) of the church at Cenchreae (Rom. 16:1). Does this mean Phoebe holds the office of deacon or minister in that church, since Paul's use of *diakonos* in other cases (Eph 3:7; Col. 1:23, 1 Tim. 4:6) presumes such standing? The question intrigues, especially given the centuries-long debate on women in ministry that continues in some quarters today. The coupling of that term with a specific congregation in this text by Paul makes the verbal gymnastics required to reject such standing far more imposing than to make an argument from this text that her vocation is indeed *diakonos*, minister.

Perhaps Paul does not fix her status in clear terms because it is not ministerial standing claimed but Christian service rendered that forms the core of his affirmation of Phoebe. That, in itself, illuminates Phoebe's witness to servanthood rooted in love. Namely, servanthood does not depend upon rank. Phoebe may have been the presiding minister (*diakonos*) at Cenchreae, the eastern seaport of Corinth, the gateway to Corinth's trade to Asia, a place—and ministerial position—of prominence. On the other hand, Phoebe might also have held no formal office in ministry. Whatever her office or lack thereof, Phoebe served and Phoebe ministered as a benefactor to Paul and many others.

Benefactors, persons willing to give of themselves to support the lives and needs of others, remain a sorely needed commodity among us. The struggling congregation in the opening story desperately needed benefactors, persons and families willing to "stand before" the financial needs of that church. None appeared, and that church closed its doors for a time. Servanthood comes in sacrifice at one's own expense, not from the desire to control or to gain privileged standing but for the sake of helping. And if example of servanthood as benefactor is needed, "I commend to you our sister Phoebe."

For Meditation This Day

Help me, O God, bear graciously the cost of service to others, even as you have borne the cost of grace for me.

Day 6

PHOEBE

An Opportunity for Others
ROMANS 16:1-2

"When was it that we saw you a stranger and welcomed you?"
—Matthew 25:38

ANY OF THE families in the community in which I now live descended from Finnish immigrants who came to the United States in the early 1900s. One story from that time tells of a young girl who emigrated alone, without parents or family to accompany her. She had only her name and destination written on a piece of paper pinned to her overcoat. Those who sent her off must have hoped that others on the journey might recognize the name or share the destination and befriend her. Did those persons ever wonder whether others would view this child as a burden or an opportunity?

Paul's commendation of Phoebe to the Roman church

intimates that she will be visiting there. Some commentators even suggest that she served as the courier for Paul's letter to the church at Rome. The fact that Paul introduces her as deacon and benefactor strongly implies that the Romans have no prior knowledge of her. Phoebe is a newcomer, an unknown quantity. All that she bears, if you will, is this bit of paper Paul has pinned to her overcoat to identify who she is and to evoke Rome's assistance by tending to her needs. "Welcome her in the Lord…and help her in whatever she may require from you" (16:2).

In this reading, Phoebe's relationship to servanthood is less one of example and more one of opportunity: Phoebe provides the occasion and person to whom the Roman church may render service. And to be a servant, after all, requires a recipient to whom one renders service.

Some who read these words may want to file immediately for that job opening: to be the one others serve. Accepting such help, however, does not always come easily. Accepting help acknowledges a need, a lack, a wanting, an incompleteness—and human pride does not always readily admit to that. Peter will have no part of Jesus' washing his feet, at least initially (John 13:8). Others of us find it very hard to accept help, whether emotional or financial or otherwise. It would be a blow to our ego, an admission of a lack of control, a sign of weakness.

So consider the one whom Paul calls on the Romans to help: Phoebe, the deacon of the church at Cenchreae, the benefactor of many and of Paul. Ministers can be notorious for refusing help, since giving help is the minister's job. Yet Paul calls on the Romans to help Phoebe the deacon. And benefactor? Phoebe has made a name and reputation for herself by being the one who supports others, the one who carries many by her wealth and generosity. But all of us, even the best of us at carrying the weight and need of others on our shoulders, need support and help from someone else. "Help her in whatever she may require."

Do the Romans practice what Paul preaches, extending welcome and help to Phoebe? The text leaves the matter unresolved. In the same way that we cannot be sure of how others viewed the Finnish girl boarding a steamer for America, we cannot know if the Romans judged Phoebe as burden or opportunity. Even so, the question is not so much their treatment of Phoebe then as how we render—and *allow*—Christian service today.

To whom do you extend welcome and help in whatever is required? Whom do you allow to help you; that is, whose service do you enable? Grace comes not only in the serving; at times it comes in giving another person the opportunity to serve. If you wonder how that can be, "I commend to you our sister Phoebe."

For Meditation This Day

May I not turn away from need where I may help; may I not turn away from help that I may need.

Day 7

MAKING
CONNECTIONS

*"Whoever wishes to be great among you must be your servant...
just as the Son of Man came not to be served but to serve."*
—Matthew 20:26, 28

IFFERENT BARRIERS define the margins from which this week's voices speak. Baruch labors within a vocation that presumes his anonymity. The woman who anoints Jesus moves in the shadows cast by her sin. Phoebe is an anomaly in her time. While Paul confirms Phoebe as a *diakonos* in the church at Cenchreae, this same Paul in a letter to Cenchreae's nearest neighbor commands women to be silent in *all* the churches (1 Cor. 14:33–36). In each case, however, those margins cannot contain their example of servanthood energized by love.

The voice of Baruch affirms that biblical servanthood does not require (nor does it promise) positions of power or renown from which to work. Servanthood does not even presume that one will be doing extraordinary acts of unprecedented creativity. Servanthood derives from being of service. Baruch copied the words of another, not once but twice. When called upon to do so, even at risk to himself, he brought those words that did not originate with him to others. Baruch left no biblical book in his name, but he conveyed the word entrusted to him. In doing so, he proved himself of service to Jeremiah and to God.

The voice of the woman who anoints Jesus testifies that "servant" is not an honorary title vested upon those designated as worthy of the honor. A servant is one who embodies love by engaging in actions of service to others, even when the one doing the serving seems unlikely if not offensive to our sensibilities. The very word *servanthood* implies humility ("servitude"), a quality that does not always come easily to those who take pride in self-accomplishment. Perhaps that need for humility sheds light on Jesus' dictum that the showing of love depends on knowing oneself forgiven. After all, bending the knee to serve may come more easily to those who have already flexed knees to receive forgiveness.

Phoebe's voice may be the most intriguing of all in her witness to servanthood. From Phoebe we hear not only the call to serve as benefactor to others but to allow others the occasion to practice servanthood in her (our) direction. Sometimes the latter can be as hard for us to accept as the former. For as critical as our rendering of service to others truly is, allowing others the chance to serve can be equally life-giving. To be of service to another person enables us—even as it can enable the one who would help us—to experience the grace of showing and accepting love.

Through the voices of all three characters, we find the ministry and identity of Jesus as servant. Clearly Jesus expended his life in service to others. But it should be noted in the story of the woman who anoints him that he allows her to serve him. Jesus' gift to this woman is not only his words of forgiveness and salvation. Preceding that gift, even embodying it, Jesus gives her the opportunity to express her love. By story's end we find ourselves asking here, Who serves whom?

The answer to that question may well be the bedrock aim of biblical servanthood. Once servanthood is embodied in love, precise lines of who serves whom become blurred. Servant and served find their lives meshed by the embodiment of love one for the other. May you find that mutuality of love true in your serving…and in your being served.

For Meditation This Day

Give me the heart of a servant, O God, that I may be found and held in love.

WEEK SIX

ᕽ

Promises

Biblical spirituality lives toward God's reign with persistence and hope. The reign of God does not come easily nor without opposition. Persistence keeps faith's shoulders to the task when resistance arises from within or without. When God's reign seems contradicted or even defeated, hope invigorates faith with the assurance that God will not disappoint. Such hope lives in expectation and as precursor of the refrain sung in Revelation 11:15: "The kingdom of the world has become the kingdom of our Lord and of his Messiah."

Day 1

SHADRACH
MESHACH
ABEDNEGO

Who Is the God?

DANIEL 3:1-18

"How long will you go limping with two different opinions?
If the Lord is God, follow him; but if Baal, then follow him."

—1 Kings 18:21

REMEMBER A STORY my sixth-grade teacher told my class. The story took place in the early 1960s, two or three years after the overthrow of Fulgencio Batista by the forces of Fidel Castro. The story went something like this: An envoy of the Cuban revolutionary government visited a classroom in a Catholic elementary school. After asking the children if they liked candy, he challenged them to close their eyes and take a test: Pray to God for a piece of candy. The children prayed to God, then opened their eyes. Nothing happened. Now, he said, offer a similar petition to Fidel Castro. When they shut their eyes and made their request in the name of Castro, the envoy placed a piece of candy on each desk.

Now whether the story stems from an actual event or arises from the anticommunist and anti-Castro rhetoric of that period in our nation's history, I cannot say. But either way, it illustrates the tension brought about by competing claims for who will serve as "God" in our lives—and why.

That same tension takes center stage in the story of the three Hebrew youths named Shadrach, Meshach, and Abednego. Set in the time of Israel's exile in Babylonia, the story begins by depicting King Nebuchadnezzar's construction of a huge, golden statue and the issuing of a royal decree for all to worship it. The fact that the king constructs the statue makes an implicit but powerful statement about how secular power may usurp the trappings of godhood for its own benefit. If a state can create a god, then who in fact is the god?

A group of Chaldeans come to Nebuchadnezzar bringing charges against three Hebrew youths who hold appointed positions in the government (3:12). Notice the order of the charges. The youths "pay no heed to you, O King. They do not serve your gods" (3:12). Disobeying the king precedes ignoring the gods. So who is more important?

The king, who earlier has had a positive relationship with the three (1:3-7, 18-20), offers them a second chance—or perhaps the better expression would be a *final* choice. Fall down and worship, or be thrown into a furnace. And just so there is no misunderstanding about who the three are up against here, he adds, "Who is the god that will deliver you out of my hands?" (3:15). The statue is not the feared adversary but Nebuchadnezzar the god-maker. What god can withstand someone who fashions gods by decree?

The three respond to the king with a twofold affirmation. The first half entrusts their deliverance to the One they serve if God is able. Deliverance is not arrogantly presumed but humbly entrusted. The second half affirms a more remarkable truth: Even if deliverance does not come—nothing changes. They will not serve the king's gods; they will not worship the king's statue. They will die with faith intact. These three have already settled the question, Who is the god? regardless of their possible fate on one given day at the hands of a would-be godmaker.

The ultimate test of Who is the god? does not weigh which power benefits us most, whether in ancient Babylonia or revolutionary Cuba or mainstream middle America. We reveal our response to the final test of Who is the god? in our choice of whom we entrust ourselves to without reservation and regardless of cost. We live toward God's reign when we exhibit the trust in God showed by Shadrach and Meshach and Abednego before entering the furnace.

For Meditation This Day

God who is, do I serve you because of what you provide me? Does my service wane when supplies run short? Help me trust who you are, above and beyond what you give.

Day 2

SHADRACH
MESHACH
ABEDNEGO

The Fourth One

DANIEL 3:19-30

When you pass through the waters,
I will be with you...when you walk through fire
you shall not be burned.

—Isaiah 43:2

HE SUSPICION OF abandonment lingers near the presence of death. Even Jesus on the cross lends his voice to pronounce the psalmist's cry of God-forsakenness (Mark 15:34; Psalm 22:1). Daniel 3 does not give insight into the final thoughts of the three Hebrew youths on the immanence of God or the lack thereof, as the furnace is fired to seven times its usual temperature. It does not reveal what they feel when cords wrap tight, binding ankles and wrists, or whether the slightest tinge of despair comes when the heat envelops them as their captors toss them into the flames. Their previous words indicate that their fate will not sway them from faith—whether God delivers them or not.

Interestingly the story from this point on does not focus on the three, even when the miracle of their not being consumed by the flames becomes apparent. Something else astonishes and confounds the king: Who is this fourth one in the furnace, the one with a god's appearance (3:24-25)? The king bids the three youths come out of the fire. The fourth one he ignores. Or does the king's fear prefer that the fourth stay there?

In any event, while the witnesses to the intended execution marvel at the untouched condition of the three, the first words out of Nebuchadnezzar's mouth have to do with the fourth one: "Blessed be the God of Shadrach, Meshach, and Abednego" (3:28). To be sure, the king goes on to assert that an angel has delivered the three. But remember the king's original ultimatum: "Who is the god that will deliver you out of my hands?" (3:15). Whether by angel or theophany, that question has been settled. God does not always dwell on high. For saving reasons, as for these three, God comes down low. God enters the fires and the waters with us to save.

In the case of Shadrach, Meshach, and Abednego, God's immanence enables them to walk out of the furnace alive and unscathed. It is not always so. Sometimes the fires burn, and the waters overwhelm, and doors close. To make this story into a proof text that God will always and everywhere deliver us on this side of life's shore would be a mistake. Such misinterpretation would do injustice to families who watch loved ones die long before their time from illness or violence. It would do injustice to those stigmatized or martyred for the sake of goodness, as if God's lack of intervention represents God's withdrawal of favor. And it would most certainly do injustice to the theology of the cross, where God in Christ enters the kiln of human hatred to fire pure grace.

God stands every bit as close to those who keep final vigils as God stands beside the three saved Hebrew youths. We cannot presume beforehand how God will act in the singular crises of personal lives and human history. Shadrach, Meshach, and Abednego do not say deliverance is sure. Whether God delivers or not, it is this God they will serve. With such faith, the three can perish in the furnace and still be accompanied by the fourth one. They enter the furnace as those determined to live toward God's reign, whether that determination lands them back in the realm of Nebuchadnezzar or forward into the realm of God.

Like Shadrach, Meshach, and Abednego, may we enter life as those determined to keep our faith with persistence and hope. May we do so, trusting in the One who will pass through the fire with us and never forsake us!

For Meditation This Day

"The soul that on Jesus still leans for repose....I'll never, no, never, no, never forsake." (From the hymn "How Firm a Foundation")

Day 3

DISMAS

The Fear of God

LUKE 23:32-41

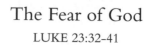

The fear of the Lord is the beginning of wisdom.
—Proverbs 9:10

 N THE NEW Testament, one pervasive theme proclaims how the grace of God's presence banishes fear— or at least intends to do so. To Mary, dismayed at an angel's greetings; to shepherds, terrified at the glory of God shining around them; to disciples, frightened by the sight of Jesus walking toward them on the waves of Galilee's sea; to women, alarmed at finding a living stranger in an emptied tomb: The word is the same, "Do not fear." A similar message appears in the early church's theological reflections: "Perfect love casts out fear" (1 John 4:18). Fear seemingly belongs to the past, a primitive remnant of a religious sentiment outgrown and outmoded by grace's appearance in Jesus.

All four Gospels agree that three men hung on crosses. None of the Gospels names the two on either side of Jesus. Apocryphal works identify the pair as Gestas and Dismas. Some scholars question whether they were mere thieves or revolutionaries. The word Mark and Matthew use for them (*lestes*) could have either meaning. Whatever the two have done, however, pales in light of what is now being done to them. Crucifixion involved a slow, agonizing death. Modern medical thought speculates that the crucified "drown," unable to expel the fluids that gradually fill the lungs.

"Are you not the Messiah? Save yourself and us!" (23:39). We might read into these words of Gestas something of a plea— or at least a dare. Luke gives us no hint of Gestas's tone of voice, although he does categorize the response as derision (23:39) that closely parallels the scoffing that sounds from the foot of the cross (23:35-36). Gestas separates himself from his fellow sufferer by ridicule.

Dismas engages a very different dynamic. "Do you not fear God, since you are under the same sentence of condemnation?" (23:40). In these words, Dismas recognizes that a community of sorts exists on Golgotha—a community of the condemned. To ridicule one who shares that same fate demonstrates, in the mind of Dismas, not bad manners but bad faith in the absence of any fear of God. Fear of God, in its most positive sense, involves the recognition of standing on holy ground. And what ground could be more sacred than the one stood upon—or impaled upon—at the closing of life, when encounter with God looms imminent?

The fear of God evokes not only Dismas's assertion of solidarity, but it elicits his confession of a glaring injustice. The fact that all three men share Rome's sentence of execution does not translate into all three equally meriting that verdict. "We are getting what we deserve for our deeds, but this man has done nothing wrong" (23:41). The fear of God that comes from standing on holy ground does not waste time in equivocation or mocking others. Instead it admits to the truth of one's own life. That admission in itself can be a fearful act, especially when owning the truth does not translate into cause for self-congratulation.

The story of Dismas awaits completion, so more than the fear of God awaits revelation on Golgotha's crest. Still the story to this point does give pause to exorcising fear of the holy completely from our spiritual journey. Fear and holiness work in tandem, reminding us that encounter with God is neither casual nor without consequence. When we stand on holy ground, knees should bend; spirits should bow; and truth should overwhelm us.

For Meditation This Day

O God, do I take you too much for granted? Have I forgotten the mystery of coming into your presence? Return me to the fear and grace of holy ground.

Day 4

DISMAS

Remember Me When

LUKE 23:42-43

Remember me, O Lord, when you show favor to your people.
—Psalm 106:4

EMEMBER WHEN…?" The words typically frame an invitation to revisit the past, to recall old places or relive former relationships. Reunions of school or family have those words and their invitation built in to the dinners, programs, photographs, and conversations that accompany such events. The longing to "remember when" may be felt even more keenly by those who live without benefit of reunion times. For them, for us, "remember when" comes then in solitude: in the flashing of a face in our minds or the hint of a long-forgotten scent or distant words we yearn—or dread—to hear again. "Remember when" revisits the past. Its curse or blessing is that remembrance cannot alter the past. Remembrance can only alter the future!

To Dismas on the cross, "remember when" in terms of times gone by evokes just cause for his and Gestas's condemnation for their deeds (23:39). This punishment does not mean that Dismas has no good memories worthy of recollection in his dying hour. The text does not address all that passed through his mind and heart regarding the past. What the text does address is the attitude of Dismas toward the future, and in particular the way in which remembrance and God's reign intersect in the person crucified beside him.

"Jesus, remember me when you come into your kingdom" (23:42). "Remember when" looks back. "Remember me when" looks forward. Luke provides no clues as to what Dismas knows of Jesus before this moment. Dismas's earlier words from the cross to Gestas assert a belief in Jesus' innocence (23:41). Dismas hears the mocking of Jesus as Messiah or Christ (23:35, 39). But a wide gulf separates hearing and trusting. To hear Jesus ridiculed as a powerless messiah now nailed to a cross does not provide incontrovertible evidence for Dismas to entrust life and destiny to Jesus. Yet Dismas does exactly that. Dismas places what life remains in the hope of God's reign. "Remember me when."

Does Dismas speak and trust out of sheer desperation? Is his faith a last-minute gambit with nothing to lose? Perhaps. Yet none of us has an exit visa from this life apart from death. So the cynical among us might deem any act of faith one of sheer desperation. All that separates us from Dismas is that we do not teeter on the brink of the abyss—we hope.

The trust-as-desperation interpretation of Dismas falls short when measured by Jesus' response. This same Jesus perceived the true need of a rich young ruler and confronted him with that need. This same Jesus saw through and called out the hypocrisy of self-righteous leaders. In other words, Jesus could spot a phony, even on a cross. But in Dismas, he sees the real thing. "Truly I tell you, today you will be with me in Paradise" (23:43). Dismas's plea for Jesus to "remember me when" finds answer not in the recollection of a past quickly dying but in the promise of a future soon rising. *Today* marks the immediacy of Jesus' vow to remember. *With me* reveals the gift and means of God's reign.

Today and *with me* still form the promise of God's reign for us. Like Dismas, may we entrust the whole of our lives and futures to the One who will remember us when time stretches beyond time—and God's reign moves from promise to experience.

For Meditation This Day

Jesus, remember me when I seek you now; remember me when my seeking ceases; remember me when I am found in you forever.

Day 5

UNNAMED FAITHFUL

Commendation and Hope

HEBREWS 11:32-40

"I have let you see [the promised land] with your eyes,
but you shall not cross over there." Then Moses,
the servant of the Lord, died there in the land of Moab.

—Deuteronomy 34:4-5

N MY COLLECTION of family photographs, I have three or four snapshots taken at the turn of the century somewhere in the South Pacific on board a ship. I have reason to believe that one of the navy men in the pictures may be a grandfather I never met. At the time of his death my oldest sister was a toddler, while my other sister and I had not yet been born. He never got to see what became of his two sons' families or the bedroom set my father made with some of the tools and the knowledge my carpenter-grandfather had passed on to him. I look at those photographs with curiosity, even as I look with hope that he might someday see what became of his family.

I look on aging church photographs with the same mingling of curiosity and hope. Men with starched collars and watch chains, women in ornate hats and skirts flowing to the ground—all frozen in time on the steps of an old white-frame building. A few names may survive but not many. A few stories may still circulate but not nearly all that once echoed in classrooms, sanctuaries, and kitchens. We wonder and hope that those long gone will see what became of their faith, witness, and service. Such wondering and hope may stem from an even deeper longing that others will do the same when our names and stories have ceased being spoken from lips and in places we now take for granted.

In this day's reading from Hebrews 11, we find the recitation of faith's exemplars shifted from names and stories we know to those that have passed into anonymity. The Bible does not tell the stories and record the names of all the people who ever trusted God. But what the Book of Hebrews does in this chapter is critical. It commends persons of faith, even when no name or particular story attaches to that commendation. The life of faith does not equate anonymity with being forgotten. All these faithful go commended, according to verse 39. Faith is never lost, its consequences never undone. The unnamed faithful remain part of the community of saints, even when photographs crack with age and stories disappear in the cracks of human memory.

The other key message this passage reveals about the unnamed faithful comes in its words that they "did not receive what was promised...so that they would not, apart from us, be made perfect" (11:39, 40). The unnamed faithful remind us that faith's journey—and fulfillment—crosses life spans and generations. Nothing we do in this life as part of our faith and service speaks the final word or accomplishes the final act. Mission and ministry always carry us forward, always await fresh vision and new understandings—and always remind us that others who follow after will complete what we've begun.

That is a humbling and liberating thought. If we set our eyes—and churches—only on those things we can complete in a lifetime, much less under five-year plans of goals and objectives, we do not see far enough. We do not reach far enough. Faith's commendation belongs not to those who wrap up everything in their lifetime but to those who pass on the promise to others who continue by God's grace and spirit.

So when I look at those old photographs with wonder and hope, I realize I am looking at myself. I am like the faces pictured there. The best of what will come of me awaits the work and faith of others who come after me. And it also awaits the reign of God, in which we will all finally come to completion in Jesus Christ.

For Meditation This Day

May I trust in you, O God, beyond the limits of what I can see and accomplish, so I may trust in you beyond life and on to life.

Day 6

UNNAMED FAITHFUL

Let Us Now Praise
ECCLESIASTICUS 44:1-15★

"Wherever the good news is proclaimed in the whole world, what she has done will be told in remembrance of her."
—Mark 14:9

HE LAST TIME I remember spending time with Lillian, we were in her daughter's kitchen. Lillian must have been nearing eighty by then, and she was laughing and chatting about her Caribbean cruise. What made that conversation all the more enjoyable was recalling fifteen years or more before, when Lillian was not Lillian but Mrs. Schaefer, the primary department superintendent in our Sunday school at Salvator Evangelical and Reformed Church.

I can still picture her before fifty or sixty of us children at the opening programs. Even in the lower elementary grades, most of us already stood as tall as Lillian. Years later, after I'd decided to enter the ministry, Lillian would remind me and others of how she always thought that's what I should do, and how she used to tell me that. But now, in her daughter's kitchen, she was having a grand old time talking about all the fun she was going to have on that cruise. Children, grandchildren, and former Sunday school pupils teased her about finding a new boyfriend. Lillian teased back in kind.

As I said, this was the last time I remember being with Lillian. In the opening weeks of my final year at seminary, Mom phoned me to relay the news of Lillian's death and the time of her funeral at the church where she nurtured the faith of several generations. The day of the service found me seated toward the back of the sanctuary by myself. What I remember most about my feelings that day was not so much the sadness that her life had come to an end but a profound sense of appreciation for her. Along with that sense of appreciation came a strong sense of assurance that Lillian's life was not lost to me or to others. The remembrance of instilled learning lingered; the hope of reunion loomed in the distance.

"Let us now sing the praises of famous men [and women]."

No monument to Lillian Schaefer rises above the St. Louis skyline. The church she and I shared has long since closed. But the words of Ecclesiasticus speak for her praise, as they speak for countless others whose names or faces may come to mind as you reflect on persons who shaped your faith. Death has not undone their work and service. Your faith testifies to that.

So why, in the last of these readings based on neglected voices from the Bible, have we moved outside the biblical witness to the Apocrypha and to Lillian? The shift underscores the movement this work intends to spark—the hearing and heeding of faith's neglected voices among us.

This book has sought to push us to a greater appreciation of characters and stories not usually remembered from the biblical witness. But faith's witness does not end with the closing of scripture's canon. Nor does faith's witness belong exclusively to the pulpit or denominational office. In kitchens, in workrooms, and in classrooms, persons continue to give voice to faith, to the priority of mission, to the humility of service. And the validation for those voices is not vested by degrees or elected offices but by the witness given to the preeminence of God's grace and love. We neglect those voices to our own detriment.

So to Lillian Schaefer and to names evoked in your memory by her story and to all those whose names have been forgotten but whose service survives in the memory of God and the life of the church—let us sing their praise and keep their faith!

For Meditation This Day

Eternal God, renew in our minds the memory of those who brought faith to us; and may we also bring faith to others.

★ Ecclesiasticus, or Sirach, is one of the apocryphal books of the Old Testament. If your Bible does not include a collection of the Apocrypha, check with your church library or pastor for one that does. You will find the Apocrypha either between the Old and New Testaments or at the conclusion of the New Testament.

Day 7

MAKING
CONNECTIONS

"Remember, I am with you always, to the end of the age."
—Matthew 28:20

LL THE VOICES—Shadrach and Meshach, Abednego and Dismas, the unnamed faithful of Hebrews and Ecclesiasticus and beyond—share a radical confidence in God's promised reign. Their convictions reverberate when the crucified Jesus declares, "Into your hands I commend my spirit" (Luke 23:46). Jesus speaks those words not from desperation at life's ending but in hope that not even the grave separates us from God. Otherwise his words do not make sense. If God's dominion does not extend beyond human lifetimes, it holds no hope. But for three youths thrown into a furnace, for a thief nailed on a cross, and for generations of faithful who have died without seeing all the promises of God fulfilled in their lifetime—trust in God's reign begets hope.

Shadrach, Meshach, and Abednego bear witness to the primacy of God's reign in the face of competing claimants to allegiance. In their case, the rival took the form of a king. In other cases any number of contenders can test trust in God's reign, not the least of which goes by the name of self-interest. Had the three Hebrew youths lived only for themselves, survival would have dictated another course. They chose, however, to live toward God's reign, regardless of the cost to self. To those whose primary ethic is looking out for number one, their choice is unintelligible. To those whose primary ethic is faithfulness to God, their choice is inevitable.

The voice of Dismas speaks of the intersection of God's reign and this present age at the moment of dying. Where others might cling to what has been, Dismas casts his hopes on Jesus' remembrance of him in a time that has not yet come to be. The other fascinating element of that intersection comes in its gracious opening of the future to those whose pasts seem closed and unpromising. For Dismas, an admitted thief deserving of capital punishment, Jesus opens paradise. To live toward God's reign in the light of Dismas's story opens one's life and hope to extraordinary renewal. What had been flawed and marked by sin finds healing and welcome. For Dismas, for us all, God's reign practices a hospitality whose name is grace.

The voices of the unnamed faithful in Ecclesiasticus and Hebrews bear testimony to how God's reign incorporates all those who have trusted God with life, destiny, and hope. In these unnamed faithful, we perhaps find the voices closest to our own in faith's chorus. Few of us will have names and stories inscribed for generations to read, study, and enshrine. But by living toward God's sovereign realm, by trusting ourselves and our destiny into the hands and grace of God, we, like the unnamed faithful of old, will find ourselves remembered in the heart of God. And remembrance there surpasses remembrance anywhere, for remembrance in the heart of God is life.

Biblical spirituality lives toward God's reign with persistence and hope. As Dismas cried out for Jesus' remembrance of him, so we would cry out for Jesus' remembrance of us. Without God's reign to promise a time and place of remembering, the cry would be pointless. We may not always see that reign clearly before us. We may not always perceive its qualities of justice, mercy, and compassion in abundance among us. But we persist in our trust, and we rely on God to make good the words of Jesus that close the Gospel of Matthew: "Remember, I am with you always, to the end of the age" (28:20).

So ends our journey among neglected voices, voices that teach us the spirituality that is alive and well in the Bible's margins — and in the margins of our own times and our own lives!

For Meditation This Day

Loving God, whose reign will come in the fullness of time: Keep my trust and hope intact as I wait for you by serving you.